A gift for the library in
honor of my step-grandfather.

Lawrence Roberts
Principal, ELHS

The CABIN
Down the Glen

ॐ

ODELL SHEPARD

Rick Sowash Publishing Company

Cincinnati, Ohio

Rick Sowash Publishing Company
338 Milton Street
Cincinnati, Ohio 45202
www.sowash.com

Printed in the United States of America

Publisher's Cataloguing-in-Publication Data
Shepard, Odell, 1884-1967
The Cabin Down the Glen/Odell Shepard.–First ed.
June 2006

ISBN 0-9762412-7-7 The Cabin Down the Glen - softcover
Library of Congress Control Number: 2006921015
1.Nature
2.Connecticut
3.Shepard, Odell (1884-1967)
4.Solitude
I. Title

First Edition

For the people of Connecticut

TABLE OF CONTENTS

FOREWORD

Odell Shepard's *The Harvest of a Quiet Eye: A Book of Digressions* is a tapestry of essays and poems loosely woven into an account of a walking journey the author made through his beloved Connecticut in September of 1926. An engaging minor classic of the literature of walking, the book brims with good, sweet things: a love of small towns and of Nature in its tamer manifestations, an appreciation of solitude, vivid sketches of people, and an abundance of gently humorous, pleasantly self-indulgent digressions into a wide variety of other subjects. It is imbued throughout with a deeply wise philosophy of optimism and serene acceptance.

Shepard wrote in a way that suggests an alternative twentieth century, the serene and pastoral twentieth century that might have been without two world wars, economic extremes, Cold War tensions, the strain of prolonged nuclear threat, over-population and the ravaging of the environment. He kept his art clean of angst and alienation. He seems to have walked and written in a twentieth-century America that was as refreshingly remote from our own as Oz or Middle Earth.

Nonetheless, he does not shy from darkness or tragedy. No fantasist, he roots his appreciation for the beauty of life in a full knowledge of its transience. His writing on any subject, happy or sad, is strikingly good, quietly dignified yet impassioned, a noble, flowing, musical prose that aspires to poetry.

Odell Shepard (1884-1967) was a professor of English literature at Trinity College, a newspaper columnist, a pianist and singer, an indefatigable walker and trout fisherman, and even, for one term, lieutenant governor of Connecticut! Shepard wrote well on an astonishingly diverse array of topics and in nearly every literary form. His biography of Bronson Alcott won the 1937 Pulitzer Prize. His novel *Jenkins' Ear*, co-authored with his son, was a highly successful Book-of-the-Month Club selection. Books on the mythology of the unicorn, Connecticut history, Shakespeare, and trout-fishing as well as essays, poems, newspaper columns and editings of other writers whose work he admired poured from his pen in the 1920's and '30's.

The best of his published writings are to be found in his masterpiece, *The Harvest of a Quiet Eye*, a book that has compelled me to repeated readings ever since I first discovered it in 1975. After reading all Shepard's other published books as well, I began to wonder if there were still in existence any of his papers through which a devotee might browse. Circumstances transpired which ultimately brought me into contact not only with Shepard's unpublished writings and but also with what remains of his circle of family and friends.

I set to music three of the poems from *The Harvest of a Quiet Eye*, and as a requirement for entering my compositions in a contest, I needed written permission to use the texts. I wrote to Mrs. Marion Shepard, the author's daughter-in-law and literary executor; she granted me the necessary permission and alerted me to Sally Gibson, who had recently completed, as a requirement for her master's degree at The University of Florida, the first thesis ever done on Odell Shepard, consulting a collection of Shepard's papers in the care of The Watkinson Library in Hartford, Connecticut. (A trout-fishing enthusiast, she discovered Shepard by reading Nick Lyons' paperback re-issue of *Thy Rod and Thy Creel*.) As soon as my schedule permitted, I went to Hartford to examine the Odell Shepard Collection.

I was very much surprised to see a listing in the Collection's index of an unpublished manuscript entitled *The Cabin Down The Glen*. Curious, I asked to see this manuscript first and, as I pored over it, I began to grow excited.

Here was a companion to *The Harvest of a Quiet Eye*, comprised, like it, of reflective essays that often end in verse. But I found that while *The Harvest of a Quiet Eye* is a vagabond's book exploring the themes of wandering and freedom, *The Cabin*

Down The Glen is the book of a settled man, and its themes are rootedness and commitment.

I arranged for a photocopy of the manuscript to be sent to me and secured letters from both The Watkinson Library (as owner of the physical manuscript itself) and from Mrs. Marion Shepard, granting me permission to edit the manuscript and to seek a publisher for it.

In The Watkinson Library, the manuscript had appeared to be complete and intact, but my photocopy arrived with a letter from Dr. Kaimowitz explaining that there were three pairs of essays and poems that, though mentioned in the Table of Contents, were not among the papers in the Shepard Collection. Furthermore, there were four other extant essays marked "Cabin", and these, though clearly intended to be part of the book were not mentioned in this same Table of Contents.

There was much to be done. If possible, the missing portions had to be recovered; the dislocated essays and Shepard's handwritten corrections had to be incorporated. Too, the manuscript was freighted with antiquated spellings, questionable hyphenations and peculiar usages, the value of which had, each one, to be weighed. I enlisted the help of several skilled people and set to work studying, editing and learning all I could about this 'new' Shepard book, *The Cabin Down The Glen*.

After years of travel in America and Europe, Shepard, who had never previously owned real estate, began, in his late forties, to feel a yearning for a place of his own. In 1929, responding to a letter from Leslie Badmington, a fellow admirer of Connecticut smitten by *The Harvest of a Quiet Eye*, he wrote from Rome, "I shall return to America, after two years of exile, in September — very homesick for the plain, sober homeliness of Connecticut.... In September or soon after I shall take up the search for a country home to serve me and my wife and son on weekends and during vacations.... What I really want is a place to which I could go at any time for a rest, stay as long as I like, rural but not uncomfortable, and interesting for its human beings as well as naturally. You suggest calling upon me after my return. Please do that, and then we can talk of many things. In the meantime, and always, let us both do what we can to preserve and defend the Connecticut we both love. 'Connecticut' is almost a symbolic name to me, as I suppose it is to you. It stands for simplicity which is not ignorant, for honesty which is not too self-conscious, for humor which is not smart or in any way tainted by New York... How I shall love to see her again!"

Badmington and Shepard quickly became fast friends and shared walking and trout-fishing excursions throughout the remainder of their lives; he is one of the two friends to whom Shepard dedicated *Thy Rod and Thy Creel* when it was published in 1930.

Shepard found the country property of his dreams on the Old Robertsville Road just outside Riverton, bought it, and had a cabin constructed there almost entirely out of native materials. Badmington built a summer place of his own not far distant, and a golden time for both families began.

All the joys of summer were harvested there, and many of these are recounted in *The Cabin Down The Glen*. But summery and sun dappled as the book is, it is also, like the glen itself, full of shadows and darkness. The themes of transience and death are never far from Shepard's mind, and one feels that a consequent desire for solitude in which to explore these themes gradually converted the property from a summer family vacation site into a hermitage. He seems to have spent a lengthy period at the cabin almost uninterruptedly alone in 1934, the probable year during which most of *The Cabin Down The Glen* was written.

It was a dark time for America as the seemingly endless Great Depression ground on, and for Shepard it also appears to have been a dark time of intense and prolonged introspection and grappling with the tragic aspects of existence. Though the outward circumstances of his life seem to have been happy enough during that period, his ruminations are often troubled by currents of bitter anger and deep sadness, and the struggle to attain serenity against these currents is the central tension of the book.

૨☛

The Cabin Down The Glen is a book about the particular reconciliation of opposites that makes for mature manhood, a state Shepard achieves by reenacting, in his own way, time and place, man's ancient connections with Nature: solitude, husbandry, and paternity.

It is a book in which simple things — bird song, a starry night, trees, spring water — are used as points of departure for asking complex questions. What is a man? How shall he become wise? How shall he regard his own youth, maturity, decline and demise? What are the signposts of a man's inward journey? How shall a man "husband" and "father" the land he loves and, by extension, the earth? These are timeless questions and Shepard chose for this book the oldest and most universally familiar of all structures in which to explore them.

The structure of the book is organic, an upward, outward spiral of thoughts and themes rooted in the writer's experience of solitude, intensified at times to the very brink of mysticism, and yet always founded upon the solid reality of a specific time and place — the early 1930's in a Connecticut cabin. Shepard's thought spreads from that dense trunk into branches of contemplation and erudition in just the way an oak tree opens up and out in its maturity. The image is not chosen whimsically; it comes from the text itself: "...it is precisely in 'growing like a tree'," Shepard writes, "that a man fulfills his manhood — that is, by solidifying his past into a support and structure for his present, and by adding every year a new ring of growth." — words as apt for the book as for the man.

To list but a few of the rings in Shepard's trunk and the branches and leaves that flower out from it, there are speculations here on language and literature, various writers and literary movements, mystical experience, religion, the organized church, Jesus, Martin Luther and Protestantism, Nature, stone walls, starry nights, music, war, death and transience, ancient philosophers both occidental and oriental, the Great Depression, greed and materialism, voluntary poverty, social and economic reform, anarchy, the masculine and feminine principles, love of the earth, love of one's own acres, love of Connecticut, the nature of a healthy patriotism, mythology, sexuality, and friendship. There are even a few eerie moments of prophecy, as when he predicts the collapse of Russian communism or foresees the effects on our nation of greatly increased amounts of leisure time "... bringing swift destruction to many and opening new horizons for a few. This will not be our choice but our destiny. It is close upon us, and we are not ready."

In one word, *The Cabin Down The Glen* is about thinking.... "to think freely — not as the member of any party, organization, institution, religion, caste, class, nation, or club, not as one having a reputation to gain or support, but simply as one man with his center inside himself, answerable to nothing but the truth... such thinking as this [is] the hardest work and the finest sport in the world."

The strongest emanation from the book is not Shepard's thought, however, but his salient personality, paradoxical yet remarkably integrated: dashing, sensitive, charming, mystical, arrogant at times, intensely opinionated and judgmental, yet redeemed by a confessional self-knowledge and wide-ranging scholarship. He rants against the middle class even while acknowledging that no one could have a more middle class origin than he and that nothing reveals this so clearly as the very ranting in which he has indulged, citing Nietzsche and Petrarch as other examples of the same phenomenon.

Shepard is very near his best when he is able to feel bemused, even through his rage and sense of separateness, at himself: "There is, in fact, something humorously pathetic in my effort to make the wild thrushes sing a human song, to find companions in squirrels and chipmunks and spiders. This is what prisoners do, not men who have been enlarged and liberated. I confess it as a fault."

The Great Depression prompts Shepard to consider concrete

matters as well as speculative ones; he asks questions which are now being asked anew in the face of other kinds of collapse: "At such a time in the world's affairs, what can a man do to help — a man who feels as I feel it his incalculable debt and obligation to mankind? Shall he add his voice to the shouters? Shall he too rush here and there? Shall he get himself elected, or wealthy, or famous, that so he may increase his 'influence?' Or might he do perhaps as well if he should strive not so much to do as to be something, since this at least is rarer and has not been so much tried in our day? Perhaps, now that all his fellows are giving their lives to action, with results that leave much to be desired, he might set forth upon the ancient adventure of thought. Now that the stupid boasters of prosperity have had their mouths stopped for a time, he might say a quiet word about inward wealth. But better and more persuasive than anything he could say would be the example of a life lived quietly with the First Things, a life resting down upon the things found true, a life delving under and soaring over the wreck of the present to the things that everlastingly endure."

The writing is superb. "Prose can hardly say more than it sings," he says and demonstrates his dictum beautifully in evocative phrases like, "the lush and fronded wealth of midsummer".

He can fashion a perfectly crafted aphorism, aptly prim, grim and dryly cynical:

"Properly to slay young men it has always been found necessary to slay trees."

When he wishes to do so, he can swing hearty, Whitmanesque rhythms: "We are close of kin to all Earth's children, born of the same wild mother, fed at her breast like them, and soon to fall asleep as they in her strong arms."

At other times he creates effects of the greatest delicacy through a wizardly use of hushed alliterations and repetitions: "The silent looms that weave the world's beauty never linger, never pause."

Single lines like these are poetry, though they be forever bound in paragraphs. Such lines echo or glow through one another when Shepard extends and sustains them, laying one over another like soft, musical chords or strokes from a painter's brush, as in this, the opening paragraph of his essay on the hermit thrush:

"Twilight is falling in the glen. Hues of pearl and amethyst are thrown back from every rock and twig and bole. Every leaf reflects a ray from the deepening west. The boughs where the shadows gather, the layered leaves, and all the expectant multitudes of the fern, are very still. Once more the trees sink into meditation, groping down that endless road of thought or dream which claims them every night and all the winter long. So still they are, so breathless, that one might think them carved in jade or painted in a picture. They seem to be holding their breath to listen."

Truly, this is prose that says what it has to say by singing.

Shepard lavished all his skill and love on this book— why was it never printed?

The Harvest of a Quiet Eye had been published in the late 1920's, at a time of great prosperity and, very likely, Shepard expected that a companion volume to that book would be welcomed. He began the writings that eventually became *The Cabin Down the Glen*, but the Depression deepened before the manuscript was completed and could find its way into print. As the decade wore on, Shepard became involved in other projects and by the time the Depression and then World War Two were over, the modest success of *The Harvest of a Quiet Eye* had probably been forgotten, American society had changed drastically, and publishers were no longer interested in books of reflective essays and poems on solitude and Nature.

Shepard eventually sold his country property and the manuscript lay in his files until after his death when it passed into the custody of The Watkinson Library. It was waiting for me there when I walked through the door in March of 1991.

XVIII

Those who assisted me were generous and effective, and I am grateful. The spellings and punctuation were rendered consistent by my mother-in-law, Mrs. Ann Ackerman, an English teacher for 25 years. Foreign quotations were translated by Dr. William McCulloh, of Kenyon College, Gambier, Ohio. Dr. Jeffrey Kaimowitz and Susan Spitler of The Watkinson Library in Hartford, Connecticut helped decipher Shepard's handwritten corrections and succeeded in locating some of the manuscript's missing sections. My friend Dan Laskin helped me devise the Foreword and Afterword. Biographical information on Odell Shepard and his years at the 'cabin down the glen' was provided by Mrs. Marion Shepard of Jordan's Cove, Connecticut, Mrs. Barbara Holden Yeomans of Newport, New Hampshire and Mrs. Mary Wood Lawrence of Williamstown, Massachusetts.

As Shepard says very near the end of this book, "Great thanks!"

Rick Sowash
Gambier, Ohio
August 9, 1991

Leap ahead almost fifteen years. *The Cabin Down the Glen* is to be published at last! And for that blessing some additional expressions of thanks are required. Fervent thanks go to Walt Landgraf of the Barkhamsted Historical Society for sharing with Rebecca Ransom the copy of the manuscript I presented him so many years before. That simple gesture started the process which finally brought about the publication of this book. Heartfelt thanks go to Ms. Ransom for her immediate interest in the manuscript and to her employer, the *Waterbury Republican American*, for allowing her to pursue the story of the manuscript's discovery. Thanks to Michael Renzullo, all grown up now, a sculptor and an architect, for his interest in the story behind the mysterious cabin down in the glen, just beyond the backyard of his boyhood home. Sincerest thanks to John Shepard, grandson and literary executor of Odell Shepard's estate, for generously permitting the book to be published. Fond thanks to my friend John Tallmadge for his encouragement and for helping me to think clearly about so many aspects of my undertaking to publish the book. Beloved daughter, Shenandoah Sowash, your proud Papa thanks you for contributing your skills as a copy-editor. Finally, thanks to my long-time friend, graphic artist Rand Wright, who designed this fine book you hold in your hand.

Rick Sowash
Cincinnati, Ohio
January 16, 2006

And thou shalt be in league with the stones of the field, and the beasts of the field shall be at peace with thee.

— The Book of Job

Beloved Pan, and all ye other gods who here abide, grant me to be beautiful in the inner man, and all I have of outer things to be at peace with those within. May I consider only the wise man truly rich, and may my store of gold be such as none but the good can bear.

— Plato's *Phaedrus*

The door is opened, and God saith to thee: "Depart." Whither? To nothing dreadful, but to the place whence thou comest — to things friendly and akin to thee, to the elements of Being... For all things are full of Gods and Powers. Whoso hath these things to think on, and seeth the sun and moon and stars, and rejoiceth in the earth and the sea, is no more solitary than he is helpless.

— Epictetus

Willst Du in's Unendliche schreiten?
Geh' nur in's Endliche nach allen Seiten.
[Do you want to stride into the Infinite?
Just walk into the Finite on all sides.]

— Goethe

Claude fenestras, ut luceat domus.
[Close the windows, so that the house may shine.]

— Henry More's motto

May those who worship thee by the light of tapers at noonday bear charitably with those who content themselves with the light of that glorious planet thou has placed in the midst of the heavens!

— Voltaire

For the first I of the man-thing was not the I of himself, but only of Us, mankind. If he danced the I-song in his loneness, it was to call to himself that Other by which he is made more completely one in becoming not himself only.

— Mary Austin

The CABIN
Down the Glen

TWENTY-FIVE ACRES

Until recent months I have never cared to own the smallest portion of the earth's surface. A few cubic feet, hollowed out for me somewhere beneath that surface when I come to "settle down," has been my sole ambition of that kind, and even this I have been willing to postpone indefinitely. It has been my pride and pleasure to go through the world like a bird that wanders widely but leaves no trail, enjoying all places the more because it owns none. Private ownership in land has seemed to me hardly defensible on grounds of reason, and even mildly ridiculous. Of course I am aware that rich men have surrounded the institution of land-holding with immemorial sanctities and have managed to give most of the rest of us an impression that the boundaries of their estates were originally surveyed and solemnly ratified by God himself; but I have always rather inclined to the opinion of Josephus, who flatly asserts — in the second chapter of his first book — that the original of all surveyors, "realtors," and perpetrators of No Trespassing signs, was Cain.

The undeveloped acres of Eden had seemed to this first millionaire merely so much real estate going to waste, for he, as Josephus reports, "was not only wicked in other respects but was wholly intent upon getting." And therefore, after he had slain his brother and had been driven from the Garden with a brand on his brow, he invented that custom, since so popular, of surrounding pieces of "property" with a fence or wall and commanding the rest of the world to keep off. But let Josephus tell it: "He did not accept his punishment in order to amend, but to increase his wickedness; for he only aimed to procure everything that was for his own bodily pleasure, though it obliged him to be injurious to his neighbors.

3

The Cabin Down the Glen

Thus he augmented his household substance with much wealth by rapine and violence; he excited his acquaintance to procure pleasure and spoils by robbery; and he became a great leader of men into wicked courses. He also introduced a change in that way of simplicity wherein men lived before, and was the author of weights and measures. And whereas they lived innocently and generously while they knew nothing of such arts, he changed the world into cunning and craftiness. He first set boundaries about lands."

No man, however, is to be held accountable for his ancestry, and I have never nourished an unreasonable grudge against the Sons of Cain. It is only that I have been unwilling to regard them as quite my social equals. I have relegated them to the submerged class of persons whose chief social function and duty it is to own things, taking my stand — perhaps too proudly — among the wanderers and wastrels who merely enjoy the possessions of others, without responsibility or care. If this has been selfish, it has caused no apparent jealousy. Even in democratic America I have never been seriously condemned, except by watchdogs, for aspiring to the ancient aristocracy of those who smile at barbed wire and cheerfully cut across lots.

But no single condition in this world comprises all possible advantages — no, not even the foot-loose condition of the land-less man. And although I still hold that the lackland wanderer is better off in most ways than the landlord, I have been obliged to admit that he falls short of full felicity in one regard: he is always either a guest or an intruder. It is true that a good and self-respecting vagabond enjoys both of these roles, and yet he would like now and then to entertain others. He would dearly like to draw about him a few persons and things of his own kind, and not to be always and everywhere merely "one of those present." He wishes, in short, to play the host, but to that end he must have a social habitation if not a name.

Before the vagabond turns landlord and gives up his un-housed free condition, however, he will of course explore rather deeply into his own innermost wilderness of wish and dream. And what does he find there? A chaos of conflicting desires; the

Twenty-Five Acres

dream of distance and the answering dream of home; a wish for endless wandering and another wish, deep as our unconscious yearning toward the grave, for one little plot of earth; longing for boundless experience and knowledge on the one hand, and, on the other, a passion to know one simple place utterly and forever; ancestral memories of nomad fathers roaming all their lives long, and clearer recollections of fathers who tilled the self-same homely acres for humdrum hundreds of years.

For, oh, it is a chaotic wilderness of dreams and wishes that each of us finds within. What wonder that it should be more than a full-time job to keep a single human being — oneself to wit — properly entertained? — a human being who demands everything at once, never considering how hard it is to combine life's opposite categories, to crush its bitter and sweet into one cup, to harmonize the wild and the tame, to unite the far and the near, to know both the great and the small!

On this excursion, inward-bound, Lackland ponders also the institution of property and asks himself what, if anything, can be said for it. He knows that for most of his contemporaries it is hedged about by an almost religious awe and is therefore not a fit subject for rational investigation; but this need not prevent a man who still retains the privileges of poverty from asking a few quiet questions. In particular, he considers property in land, to which a quite special sanction has been attached for thousands of years, for which most wars have been fought and most laws framed, upon which most of the baser and commonly recognized aristocracies have been founded. And yet to him, at least, it is one of the oddest whimsies ever hatched in a human brain — this notion that merely by tendering and recording bits of written paper a man may come to "own" a portion of our planet and to call it his, forever! If he had fought for that land at the risk of his life, if he had made it habitable by destroying beasts or by draining a swamp or by cutting it free from the forest, then one could see some meaning in his ownership; but merely to transfer written paper from one bank-account to another — a thing that a mere fine lady might do, or a mere rich man, or any anemic literary person

The Cabin Down the Glen

who could not even hold an axe or a gun! — no vagabond can
hope to comprehend this. It is to him only one more example
of the elaborate hocus-pocus by which our amusing world-let
is managed, a rather tedious and trivial kind of child's play.
Common sense tells him, first of all, that "the earth is the Lord's,
and the fullness thereof," and that a short and shadowy lease
is granted to those few of us who delight to walk about in it
for a while and take its wonder into our hearts before they are
stilled forever and earth swallows them. Something deeper than
common sense reminds him that we can never own any portion
of earth, even the trifling handful that we call our bodies and
that seems for a time to do our bidding, because it is earth,
no less, that surely and indefeasibly owns us.

But although Lackland does not admire this paltry make-
believe, he has to live with it. For observe how the thing works
out. Those who have acquired lands by the curious method of
interchanging written paper have put fences and walls round
them, and inside these walls and fences they have installed
sundry dogs of the more snobbish and plutocratic breeds.
The very trees, once the friends and confidants of the vagabond,
now warn him harshly in bold black lettering that "Trespassers
will be Prosecuted." Whither shall he turn? Along most of the
country roads that once opened vistas into blessed solitude
these paper-passers and their like have become to him a stench,
a din, and a danger. Verily, the children of darkness are wiser
in their generation. They are crowding him off the earth which
was his home, filching that inward peace which was his only
wealth. Twist and turn as he may, there is no escaping them
— unless by following their absurd example. In order to save
a little freedom, it appears that he must give up a great deal
more. If there is to be any place where he will be neither guest
no intruder, he too must tender a bit of written paper to some
landlord, in the conventional way, and so become a landlord
himself — no less. (And soon, perhaps, no more!)

Twenty-Five Acres

For these reasons, and a few others, I have purchased twenty-five acres — "more or less" — of wild land in western Connecticut. I am already a landowner at least in name, and the vagabond in me is already undergoing subtle transformations. If this is inconsistent with my earlier professions and conduct, why then it is all the more human; but a desertion from the dwindling ranks of wanderers on foot I insist that it is not. I am retaining full and active membership in the old aristocracy, so sparsely represented in America, of those who still possess both legs and eyes. The main difference made by this recent legal transaction is that I now wander abroad less than I used to do and concentrate far more. It is a difference of scale, mainly — always to the thoughtful man, a negligible one. All that I have done is exchange mountains for molehills, and I find that these serve my turn just as well.

Those who think of landowning in terms of personal possession might feel that twenty-five acres are not enough, but for me they are sufficient. One breather can hardly exhaust all the clean blue air that bathes twenty-five acres, and, even if that were possible, there is a constant dispatch of fresh supplies from the northern slopes of the Berkshires. My land comprises meadow, woodland, laureled hillside, glen, running water, many springs, a host of trees, boulders, nations of fern, armies of wild-flowers, birds, beasts, insects — all in fact, that any reasonable vagabond could desire. One can stand in the middle of it and shout poetry at the top of his lungs, and yet be heard by none of the worthy people who do not understand either poetry or shouting but only by the softly applauding hemlocks. One can walk all day mother-naked there without exciting unusual attention from the thrushes or squirrels. One can get so thoroughly lost in those twenty-five acres as to think that he is once more a homeless wanderer, gaily trespassing upon some rich man's property. Getting lost on my own land is, in fact, one of my pleasantest occupations, and one that will not soon pall.

So much for the mere surface of the land; but I should like to have it understood — and I do hereby serve notice

7

The Cabin Down the Glen

to all and sundry to whom this letter patent may come
— that I have bought a property extending in more than two
dimensions. It reaches down precisely to the centre of our
terrestrial globe, at which point it abuts, I believe, upon
the property of a Chinese rice-grower. Furthermore, at the
nethermost boundary I am next-door neighbor to every other
landowner on earth — a thrilling thought, and, to a man with
my past, a somewhat disquieting one. I find that my land is
shaped like an enormous funnel. Starting from its point at
the centre of the earth, where Dante put poor Judas between
me and the Chinese paddy-grower, it enlarges steadily in
circumference until its cross section attains an area of twenty-
five acres at the surface of the earth; and beyond that plane
it continues to expand forever, so as to include, without
cramming, the orbits of several quite respectable stars.
All things considered, though I have long been accustomed to
plenty of elbow-room, I do not feel pinched for space.

If a man born and bred a wanderer is to own land at all,
it should be the kind he has formerly liked, good for aimless
roving and open to all other vagabonds whatsoever. His barbed-
wire fence should sag in convenient places; there should be
frequent gaps in his stone walls; and of course there should
be no dog to discourage trespassers or to harry the more sensitive
inhabitants. He need not hope that the apples and blueberries
growing on his own land will ever taste so sweet to him as
those he has found on the domains of other men; yet these
arrangements should break the shock of change. They help
to preserve some vestiges of his old freedom while reaching
doubtfully forward toward the new.

No man, I feel sure, has ever held land more tentatively
than I shall hold it, or with a keener sense of the humor
involved in holding it at all. No one has ever allowed twenty-
five acres to go more serenely their own sweet way than I shall
allow these that are so charmingly called mine. What I have
"bought" is only the right to stand and look and listen while the
seasons shift their scenery on certain New England hillsides.
So much I might have done, certainly, as a landless man, but

Twenty-Five Acres

in that good condition I could never have been sure that these hillsides, this glen, this brook would not some day be tragically and murderously "improved." I could not have played the host to drifting milkweed and thistletuft, to bluebirds and squirrels and hermit thrushes, to foxes and deer and woodchucks, to orchids and cardinal flowers, and to the rare human beings who have made their peace with these creatures and mean to keep it. Now I can, now I shall. "Though much is taken, much abides." I am content.

But "content" is a cold, a dull, a merely cautious word, for the thrill that sweeps through me, as though from the earth itself, when I set my bare foot upon these acres after a separation, or when I see them darkly uplifted against the sky while walking on some distant hill. There is a mysterious ecstasy here that I did not bargain for, an obscure and nameless delight that will make me more tolerant of landowners from this day forth. Sometimes I liken myself to a man who, after many amatory adventures, finally marries the one woman of his choice, and so finds peace at last. Yes, it is like that, this feeling; but just what it is in origin and essential nature I cannot make sure, although the guess keeps recurring that there may be some faint prophecy in it of my final rest in a still smaller plot of ground. Even twenty-five acres will then be a world too wide — and it may be that when my love of earth is reduced to this sharp and final focus, "content" will seem an even colder and duller word.

In the meanwhile, I cannot too heartily approve of the preparation for my brief tenure. Had I been one of the most heavily encumbered of those who own things instead of the most carefree who merely enjoy them, these preparations could not have been more elaborate. They have been going on for a long time, with never a moment's pause.

My land — for I delight in using that humorous phrase as often as it can be made to seem appropriate! — lies in the midst of one of the earth's oldest mountain chains, in comparison with which the Alps and Himalayas and Andes are yesterday's upstarts. A glacier worked hard at it for

9

The Cabin Down the Glen

a long geologic age, and to good and manifest purpose, melting down two huge drumlins to defend me from the north wind. It gouged me a glen where the voice of living water sings beside my cabin, dropping mighty boulders about to nurse the ferns and to stand as isles of blue among the green. Earthquakes have pushed and heaved and shaken themselves so that my many springs of water might gush between the snapped and tilted granite. The frost, that doughty smiter, has labored here through more seasons than there are leaves on all the trees. And when I think of those leaves themselves, of the endless labor of leaves going back to the age of the coal levels, I bow my head with a sense of utter unworthiness. There come times when I feel overwhelmed, like a guest for whom too much has been done. There are times when I say: "Let me only look on, my brothers! Help me not to feel an intruder even here! Let me rest my hand for a moment on the boulder and feel its slow strong pulse — this hand that yesterday was only a blowing dust, and that will be whirled away tomorrow on another wind. Lend me for an instant the illusion of permanence in a world where nothing lingers. Give me a heartbeat of time in which to learn the secret of your patience, of your confidence, of your sober joy — and all the childish humble babble of 'ownership' shall be a jest between us."

Neither can I too heartily admire the huge dome that has been arched over my little plot of Connecticut — its colors and distances and lighting arrangements. Two great lamps are burning there, and smaller ones innumerable. I can lie out from dawn to midnight on one of my hills among the fern, watching hues grow and change and fade above me, without wishing for any other entertainment, without thinking one clear thought, without remembering the past or probing the future, wholly absorbed in the wonder of drawing down those incalculable miles of space, with all their shining inhabitants, through the tiny gateway of the eye.

And then there is the infinite silence, made vocal by the hermit thrush, breathing in the hemlocks, and spreading the peace of afternoon round the song of the white-throat.

Twenty-Five Acres

A good many silences I have heard here and there, some terrible and some kindly, but none like this that sings and broods all year about me. There are eight thousand miles of quiet beneath my land, and infinite reaches of quietness above it. There is, in fact, God's plenty of this good thing which I had come to suppose was growing rare, and for which I have perhaps an unusual liking.

As for guests, not one ugly thing shall I entertain and not one raucous noise. My acres lie open to all the birds of all the sky, and I judge that most of them have found it out. They are entirely free to every tattered and weatherbeaten wandering man such as I used to be, providing only that he does not carry a gun. Furthermore, I intend to gather me a company of thoughts and moods which I have never been able to spend enough time with — my own thoughts, for better or worse, and moods so shy and vanishing that only in a quiet place like this will they ever return. And finally, odd as it may sound in the telling, I expect to continue certain interrupted conversations with an elm tree and to learn what hemlocks have to say. Also, I hope to revive the little knowledge I once had of the ancient lingo spoken by brooks.

These studies, and my constant duties as a host, are likely to fill the greater part of my time; but yet I do not intend to ignore the question that some of my acquaintances have already asked: "What sort of crops are you going to grow?" The soil is so rich and the climate so propitious that I see no reason why I should fail to raise a small crop of ideas every year. (A small crop, I say; for it would be absurd to attempt anything on a grand scale, and certainly I do not intend to be industrious. At any rate, there will always be enough for my own consumption.) My hemlocks yield nobility without cultivation and the birches produce abundant harvests of humor. I expect to gather strength from the boulders, laughter from the brook, and patience from every plant and spear of grass. Certainly, then, these are fertile acres, and I wholly disagree with the farmers round about who tell me that no man can make a living off them.

The Cabin Down the Glen

Already the trees are beginning to teach me. If I must strike root, at least I shall spread great boughs against the blue where the winds are wandering and the clouds idle by. Two kinds of freedom there are — the rooted and the rootless; and no one man can say which is better or that a tree has less than a bird. There is the wisdom that comes of going forth to meet the world and another wisdom that comes of standing still. The West has one liberty and wisdom, expansive, exogenous, masculine; but the brooding East has another, restringent, retractile, feminine. The man who is deeply wise and wholly free has both.

RECOLLECTION

I must forget awhile the mellow flutes
And all the lyric wizardry of strings;
    The fragile clarinet,
Tremulous over meadows rich with dawn,
      Must knock against my vagrant heart
      And throb and cry no more.

For I am shaken by the loveliness
And lights and laughter and beguiling song
    Of all the siren world;
The regal beauty of women, round and round,
      The swift, lithe slenderness of girls,
      And children's loyal eyes,

Hill rivers and the lilac fringe of seas
Lazily plunging, glow of the city nights
    And faces in the glow —
These things have stolen my heart away, I lie
      Parcelled abroad in sound and hue,
      Dispersed through all I love.

I must go far away to a still place
And draw the shadows down across my eyes
    And wait and listen there
For wings vibrating from beyond the stars,
      Wide-ranging, swiftly winnowing wings
      Bringing me back mine own.

So soon, now, I shall lie deep hidden away
From sound or sight, with hearing strangely dull
    And heavy-lidded eyes.
'Tis time, O passionate soul, for us to go
      Some far, hill-folded road apart
      And learn the ways of peace.

THE CABIN DOWN THE GLEN

Witch hazel peers in at one window, pine branches drowse at another, and over the roof a huge rock-maple towers, brushing the shingles with pendulous twigs. Farther off, but all within one hundred feet, stand elms, wild cherries, hornbeams, birches black and yellow and white, young cedars, trembling aspens, and many hemlocks. The ground is everywhere covered with ferns in orderly masses, ferns vivid in sunlight and dark in shadow, swaying gently in the long slow drone of air that moves all day up the glen, or standing motionless as though painted in a picture. Shadow and sunshine shaken together, gleam and gloom intermingled and deepening each into the other, golden light probing the leafy recesses and laying robes of glory on tufted moss and fallen pine needles, shimmer of gold that shifts from leaf to leaf, and gold that sleeps in a pool of fern fronds — such is the scene from the cabin windows, always the same yet always changing, while the sun strides over the tree tops.

And at night when the moon comes walking there, she floods the familiar glade with a mysterious alchemy, changing the gold to silver.

The cabin itself is made of hemlock and is so engulfed and washed round and whispered over by numberless leaves that one comes to think of it as merely another tree, a huge commodious trunk of hemlock with openings to let in the daylight. It is not an intruder or even a guest in this company of trees but belongs here by as good a right as the boulder on which it stands. The light of morning rests upon the rough rocks of its chimney, still spotted with lichens, as though they had never been lifted from the glen below, and the level beams of sunset sift through the pine and lie as warmly red on it's

The Cabin Down the Glen

hemlock slabs as they do on the trunk of any living tree. Birds and squirrels, chipmunks and deer find it merely another growth of the fecund and multiform forest. The mother partridge brings her covey to feed beneath its windows.

Birds flutter about the cabin eaves and sing from its chimney top and ridgepole with no suspicion that it has been here less long than the boulders. Chickadees come in voluble troops to the witch hazel boughs and scramble and chirrup and flit there within arm's reach of the window. Then arrives a bevy of warblers, less loquacious but no less sociable, or a contingent of cedar waxwings fills the woods with vague high sibilance. Hermit thrushes sing all day farther down the glen where the shadows are deeper, and the white throat lifts a silver flute at intervals in the laurel thicket. Now and then a solitary vireo peers shortsightedly among the leaves beside the window. At noon sounds the swift shrill volley of notes that is the oven bird. A mourning dove ponders its woe, far away. In the closing weeks of summer the very voice of the glen is that of the wood peewee, distant, plaintive, summing up the stillness of the afternoon on one long sliding phrase.

When no bird sings, the air is filled with the humbler music of crickets and grasshoppers, tree toads and cicadas — a music seldom attended to until it ceases suddenly after a night of frost. And yet how comforting it is, and how much it adds to the homeliness of the American woods; those know who have listened for it vainly in some foreign land. These creatures play the ground bass in every woodland orchestration, and they play it not only all day long but far into the night. The slow and silvery song of the katydid rings on and on through the darkness. Without the steady croon of crickets, grasshoppers, cicadas, tree toads and katydids the cabin would be a lonelier place. It hums and rings with their tiny timpani. While one sits there reading a book or following some stream of revery, their music steals into every thought and mood — an undersong of quiet contentment as though to say that in its basic and simplest elements life might be good to live.

Still more pervasive is the music of leaves, ranging from

The Cabin Down the Glen

low to high, from swift to slow, and seldom ceasing. One gets to know the voices of individual trees. The deep and sober bass that sounds from the west when the cabin door is open comes from the giant pine, one hundred feet away, whose upper boughs catch many moving airs that never drop into the glen. That high exalted chattering, most audible when other leaves are still and when no otherwise discernible breeze is astir, can come from nothing but the little aspen. There is a special sound, too, of wind moving through masses of fern, and a peculiar voice of the hemlock, given forth in sombre monotone when the tree is roused from revery. All these are as characteristic as human voices. The pine could not speak in any other tone, having such mighty and long-considered thoughts to convey, nor could we expect the trivial aspen to chant with his magniloquence.

One sits in the cabin down the glen as though in a sheltering tree, unheard and unseen, watching and hearing the summer day and night go by. The gray squirrel comes head-first down the elm and sets out on mysterious errands among the ferns; the woodchuck blunders in from the meadow and explores along the brook; a chipmunk emerges suddenly from nowhere and surveys the tumbled fern forest from the rock; a dragonfly tacks and steers up and down. Such incidents are events to the watcher at the cabin window, any one of which may launch him on long voyages of thought. Even the floating strand of gossamer or the ball of thistle tuft that twirls down through the still afternoon is enough to catch and hold his attention, for these too are creatures of the place, natives here, not to be ignored.

So much for outward sights and sounds streaming in by window and doorway — but what of the inner events? For there is the test by which we may know whether this retirement is a charge or a retreat. By the depth and height and vigor of the thinking done here the question must finally be decided whether the man who lives in the cabin alone is still pulling his weight in the boat of the world or has merely skulked aside in weariness or disgust. Forty miles away a modern city rushes

16

The Cabin Down the Glen

and roars. There the news of the world is gathered, weighty business is transacted, a state is governed, goods are produced and transported and sold. Here in this quiet glen, surrounded by sheltering hills and screened by leaves, a man sits all day alone. For a time he has sidestepped the world. At a very slight cost of effort and rejection he has won the rare boon of quiet and the inestimable boon of leisure. He may say and think what he pleases. His engagements are with the dawn and the sunset. The work he does is of his own choosing.

The quiet of the glen has hushed this man so that he needs less and less in the way of outer events to keep moving the stream of his thoughts. By learning to ask for little he has gained more than most men know how to ask. He is growing outward and sinking inward at the same time. He stretches up and reaches down like a tree. For, in spite of Ben Jonson's assertion to the contrary, it is precisely in "growing like a tree" that a man fulfills his manhood — that is, by solidifying his past into a support and structure for his present and by adding every year a new ring of growth. And this man is like a tree in other ways. He feels almost as a piety his utter dependence upon the earth. He has lost the wish to wander, realizing that his destiny may as well be worked out here as anywhere. His moods of ecstasy spring up like the hemlocks, after long pauses. He is trying to recall the secret of the hermit thrush — and, even beyond that, simpler and more elemental, the meaning, faith, or confidence that underlies the cricket's croon.

But need this mean that he does no work at all? Some of the most valuable and necessary tasks before us are such as the world cannot possibly imagine, and so cannot order and direct, until they are performed. Much of the most necessary and valuable work ever yet done has been so remote from the world's conscious needs that it has been performed either in solitude or else in the face of bigoted obstruction and of ridicule.

This man has not come here, at any rate, in a holiday mood. If he seems to retreat, that may be only his method of advancing. In one way or another, but at least in his own way, he will strive to perform his share of our total effort. Possibly

The Cabin Down the Glen

his mere gesture of withdrawal may have some value for others, but that is not of his concern. He knows that the beginning of any difficult task is always a process of simplification, and that this is most true in a time superficially complex, like our own. First of all, then, he aims to simplify his life and so to concentrate his energy.

One wholly idle and relaxed, self-indulgent, or resting between two periods of activity might find all he sought here by merely sitting on the bare boulder day after day, watching the play of light among the ferns and listening to the song and whispering of the place. What, then, is the cabin for? Partly, to be sure, it serves to house a man who can never be close enough to trees until he feels almost one of them, but chiefly it serves to capture and enclose thoughts. For dreaming the horizon will do, but for thought one needs four walls and a ceiling, and therefore is it said in the *Ancren Riwle*: "Love your windows as little as possible, and see that they be small." Thought slips away and loses itself and does not come back again when the eye is set free in a wide landscape. There is such a landscape, many miles wide and deep, to be seen from the hill that rises just behind the cabin, but the hill hides all that splendor of tumbled mountains from the cabin windows. They face toward the glen, hardly seventy-five feet across, rimmed by rocks and screened by many trees. In the cabin, therefore, thought must turn inward and explore the inner landscape. And it happens to be in that interior country that this man's task awaits him.

Only a part of the world's necessary work is best done in roaring and rushing cities; some of it may be better done in glens. Only a part of our human effort is put forth most advantageously in mansions and business offices and laboratories; some of it may get better results in cabins. There are tasks, not the least important, that will never be undertaken at all unless in quiet and leisure. For these tasks there is little competition just now in America, or in the western world. Enough of us are working like engines and striving to keep the pace set by machines. We can afford to let this man work quietly, storing his strength within, like a tree.

THE HERMITAGE

Remote from any noise of men,
Hid half-way down the ferny glen,
A hemlock cabin stands alone
Beside a gray gigantic stone.
Round it, the multitudes of leaves
Make music all day long; its eaves
Are brushed by pine; the lintels drowse
Under long-layered maple boughs;
Each chimney stone and step and sill
Is green and gray with lichen still,
Is unawakened from the sleep
Its brothers in the brook-bed keep.
The wild airs wandering out and in
Encounter only their ancient kin,
And fragrance from the forest blown
Meets odor of meadows newly mown.
There time stirs not the lily's bell
And only the sloping shadows tell
Of how the gold hours come and go.
Far up the hawk, far off the crow
Patrols the boundaries of hush;
Far down the glen a hermit thrush
Sacres the temples of green shade
With holiness his song has made.
There Eden breathes; there every tree
And stone remembers Arcady;
And there may one far-wandered heart
Find all it seeks: a place apart;
A haven for all wavering wings,
The endless song that quiet sings,
Long thoughts, deep hopes, and still delights
Through golden days and silver nights.

WHILE THE MASTER SLEPT

Some hours after midnight a ray from the waning moon trickled down through the pine tops and slanted in at the cabin window. It found an old walking stick in a dim corner there, and glimmered faintly on the smooth-worn handle. Always a light sleeper and ready at a moment's notice to be up and out and away, the stick dreamed at first that it was swinging high again in the moonlight on the English ash where it once grew. Then it awoke. Peering and listening through the dusky almost silent room, it saw nothing but a bed and a chair and a table, heard only the quiet breath of the sleeper who lay unseen.

"What a dull and dismal lot for me to come down to!" sighed the walking stick. "What a slug-a-bed life for a bough that has waved in the breath of Bristol Channel and looked down on the Forest of Dean! Since the master bought me in the High Street of Oxford, I have whistled my way many times along the green spine of the South Downs; he and I have lingered together in the huge beechen shadows of Savernake and have leaned against the mighty monoliths of Avebury. I know London, Paris, Rome, Florence, Cologne, Boston, New York. I have swum in a gondola. Sussex and Surrey and the Cotswold Hills I have measured from end to end, stepping them off side by side with his left leg and swinging with his right. I know how the sunshine sleeps on the three-thousand-year-old walls of Fiesoli. I remember the roar of the Sabine cataract that Horace heard, and the shout of the River Sorgue as it rushes through Petrarch's Vaucluse. But now that old glory has all departed. In these latter days we walk among hills unfamed and by streams unsung. Where once we traveled miles we now creep rods, and instead of scaling mountains we probe anthills. Something I cannot quite make out has overcome his delight

While the Master Slept

in wandering. Distances were nothing to him in the good old days, and now they are nothing in another sense. For weeks on end we hardly cross the boundaries of these few acres; for hours at a time we pace up and down one crooked rocky path beneath the hemlocks. Longer than ever we did to the glorious cuckoos and nightingales of my youth, we stand listening to the undistinguished whitethroats and hermit thrushes of Connecticut. A walking stick must not be expected to understand such things, but I say that something has happened to him — perhaps old age. And something is happening to me. During the long hours of day and night when we are not walking, I have to stand here chock-a-block with a dull collection of untraveled wood — merely so much local oak and hickory and hemlock, utterly ignorant of the outer world and devoid of conversation! I know how Ovid felt among the Goths."

Toward the end of these remarks the walking stick had spoken, because of its indignation and self-pity, somewhat more audibly than at first. The bed, the chair, and the table overheard, and for some minutes they considered in silence what had been said. At length, murmuring drowsily in tones so low as not to disturb the sleeping man, the bed replied for all three:

"Our foreign friend may well consider that he has come down in the world after such travels as he has hinted, and it is entirely natural that he should find us dull companions. For what he says of us is true. We have never seen anything of the world except this lonely glen. We grew here, and it has always been our notion that a tree should stand where its seed first fell, that it should gaze serenely out at the far horizons but never try to cross or to change them. The wisdom of trees and their duty, it has seemed to us, consists in standing still where they are, letting the world come to them when it will or must. And I, the bed, have discovered that early or late the world does always come. For see, I bear at this moment a burden — the feet that are weary of wandering and the weary quiet hands. The wisdom of trees is in waiting. In patience is all their strength."

21

The Cabin Down the Glen

And then said the hickory chair: "What the bed has meant to suggest by his gentle and drowsy remarks, no doubt, is that our English visitor may be a bit too energetic, not to say restless or strenuous. There is a time for work, as I should know at least as well as the walking stick and perhaps better than the bed, and then there is also a time for sitting by the fire. In neither of these sensible occupations is a walking stick of much use. A little motion here and there — say from the table to the fireside and back again — is entirely allowable to trees, but this one-legged stalking up and down Europe and the British Isles strikes me as in the highest degree absurd. Ash trees may bring up their branches to that sort of thing if they like, but I am happy to say that it seldom happens among hickories."

All this while the table had been waiting massively by the window, hearing everything and saying nothing; but when the chair began to grow personal, it took the first opportunity of entering the discourse. "I think we should be unwise," it said, "if we allow this interesting conversation to degenerate into unfriendly comparisons between the different species of trees, to say nothing of comparisons between different countries. My own experience suggests to me that almost any piece of wood will do what it is made to do by our masters. As you all know, I am composed of oak and hemlock, and I assure you that nothing was more remote from the expectations of the several trees on which I grew than that they should furnish a table at which a man would sit and work; yet here I am, oak on top and bark hemlock on the sides and legs. Yes, emphatically, we are what we are made, and we perform the tasks we are set to. But I would have you all observe that there are now four theories before us concerning the strange creature whose low breathing we can all hear while we speak. The walking stick is convinced that he is, or ought to be, nothing but a wanderer; the bed regards him as a sleeper merely; the chair as a dreamer by the fire; but I know him as a man who does hard work. Now, which of us serves him best, has most of him, comes nearest to his real nature? Who shall decide?"

On the table there was lying a penholder of cherry wood.

22

While the Master Slept

The red-brown bark on it was dimly lustrous in the moonlight, for it had been polished by years of daily use. Having far more to say in this little controversy than any other piece of wood in the room, it had reserved its word until all the others had spoken. Then it began:

"Each of you seems to me entirely correct according to your experience and in proportion to your respective knowledge. Allow me to suggest, however, that none of you has fully realized how different the master is from trees and wood. We have always the same few needs and moods; we think the same thoughts year in and year out. Do you not remember that while we were still green and growing we merely rehearsed in winter what we had learned in the spring and summer months? Do you not recall how deliberate our cogitations were and how slowly we changed, even on a breezy day, from one mood to another? Well, with him it is not so. His wishes vary from hour to hour, his thoughts from minute to minute, and his needs are diverse, even contradictory. Here you have the reason why the walking stick supposes he is always at leisure, while the table thinks that when he is not laboring he must be wasting his time. The chair, knowing him a little better, fancies that if he is not sitting at the table he has nothing to do but to sit by the fire, and the bed is inclined to wonder what he does with himself when not lying at full length as he is doing now.

"These mistakes are due to the wish we all have to serve him constantly according to our power; but we must try to understand that he is more changeable than we are. He needs work and routine, and there the table serves him; but also he needs wandering and play, which gives the walking stick its chance. Furthermore — and here is a mystery that wood cannot comprehend — he needs rest. That is why he turns to the chair and the bed. Let us not fail to see, at any rate, how in every mood and in every need he turns to us. Almost on the day of his birth he was laid to rest in a hollowed tree; tonight he sleeps in another one — for what is this cabin else? — of his own choosing; and there must be now a green elm somewhere that will hold him close at last.

The Cabin Down the Glen

"I say these things not to read a lesson to pieces of wood far more massive and aged than I, but merely to give you the benefit of my experience. For some reason that has no bearing upon my worthiness he seems to confide most of all in me. You may be surprised to hear it, but the fact is that he and I have traveled much together, although we make our journeys on paper rather than over land and sea. Nudged and pushed and drawn by a human hand — a marvelous thing, most delicate and powerful and compelling — I too have gone my miles on one leg, like the walking stick. And I have learned on these travels that he has two apparently conflicting impulses: one toward roving as the winds do and one toward standing like a tree. Let us be glad that just now the mood of the tree is on him, and let us serve him as we may."

When the penholder had ceased to speak, there was a silence in the cabin until the moon had sunk behind the pine trees and dawn was pale at the window.

RAIN ON THE ROOF

A million little silver feet are dancing delicately to the music of the wind three yards above my head. At every moment their rhythms and their figures change, their tempo changes from slow to swift, from allegro to a stately-stepping andante. The room is resonant with their tiny tramplings. It reverberates like a great hollow drum under numberless muffled drumsticks.

How instantly the sense of shelter, one of the oldest of human emotions, is lifted to the pitch of glee by this patter of rain-drops! The breath-catching delight that our forefathers felt, many ages ago, in huts of piled stone roofed with boughs, when they heard the many feet of the rain just above them and knew that they were warm and dry — this comes back to us in force today, after all our centuries of comparative comfort. Probably there is no other feeling in which we come closer to them; none that carries us nearer to a realization of those interminable centuries during which the weak and naked human animal held out somehow, kept alive and not quite hopeless, against wet and cold and hunger and darkness and the creeping terrors of the dark. Shelter! Four walls and a roof that shed the rain, that break the wind, that keep the warmth in and the wilderness out! Have we forgotten how good these are? Divorced and estranged from the elemental, ignorant or forgetful of the long effort by which the simplest of our comforts have been won, have we lost for a time almost completely this ancient sense of shelter? When the dance of silver feet begins along the roof, we remember again those ages that have no history except such a revived writing on the palimpsest of the heart.

Foxes have holes in the earth and the birds have nests where they rear their young, and why should a man's dwelling be less natural than theirs? To me, at least, this revelry on my roof brings the sky and the outer world more near, even while it deepens the

The Cabin Down the Glen

sense of seclusion. I am closest to Nature while walking in the rain or against a driving storm of snow, but the present experience comes next to that. It makes me feel no longer a spectator. I am in the workshop.

For this is what I am thinking: a minute ago the raindrops now musical above me were riding high over hill and forest, playfellows of the wind. What journeys they have made in coming here, and how long they have been on the way! — sinking down to the rocky bases of the planet, lying still there in the dark for weeks or months or years, bubbling forth again to the light in springs of the mountain and of old worn pastures, washing the roots of grass and trees, climbing to the stem of a brier rose to issue in the breath of a blossom, shining in the dawn as dew, sparkling in brooks and darkling in rivers, tossing on the sea, drawn up into clouds and blown over deserts and farms and cities — and then falling at last with a dance and song to cheer a solitary man. Every drop that I hear, though young as the morning, is also very old.

I think how the summer shower will bring refreshment to this gray pasture and to that ferny lane, to the thirsting columbines on their rocky knoll and to the browning meadows by the stream. I imagine the swift patter of drops on the leaves of the maple or dimpling the surface of the lake. I see how they will glisten in the feathered grass and deep in the hearts of roses when the sun shines again. Thus the rain that shuts me in may really set me free. Fancy spreads her wings when she hears this music. The space and freedom of the day are brought into my cabin.

But the sound of this elfin drumming is best to hear when I am falling asleep. Not only does it assure me of safety but it leads my thought away until it is lost in the land I knew when a child. I may have supposed I should never come there again — for a long way it is and winding, with many intricate turns among the shadows — yet I can still win back to that land on any night when the rain is on the roof. No guide can lead me to a fairer place or to one I have longer loved. There is no faint memory of childhood that the rain has not kept fresh. And while I am listening to it, no rich man in the world is lulled by a more somnolent music. No king falls asleep to a drowsier minstrelsy.

HAYSTACK

From dawn to dusk we tossed and grappled
The meadow grasses, cloud-bedappled,
And rode them homeward, we four men,
In groaning wagon loads; and then,
Beneath the barnyard's oldest oak,
We built a new house.
           Gray as smoke
Its airy beams and rafters shoulder
Against the sundown's golden smolder;
Its bulk looms huge; its angles strange
Work on the sky so swift a change
The stumbling farm horse hardly knows
What way his road to stable goes,
And mousing owl and veering swallow
Must find new paths of air to follow.

Now stands the meadowful of clover
We saw at dawn — by bees hummed over,
By winds caressed, or rolled in billows
Down to the blowing brookside willows —
All still and dark.
           Man cannot build
Another house more silver-silled,
More beautiful when day is done,
Better for stars to gaze upon.
Here sleep the voices of the wind,
Rich attars that the bees have binned,
And lights and colors of the sky,
Blue flagons of the butterfly,
Bobolink-laughter, cricket-croon,
And all the honeyed warmth of June.

But houses made of grass and flowers
And wind song are not wholly ours.
What suns have dawned, what dews have lain,

What thunders rumbled up the rain,
Before those million blades could drowse
Beneath the shelter of oak boughs!
How tenderly the moon, tonight,
Will wash them in her silver light!

LIVING ALONE

"The door is open, and God saith to thee, 'Depart!' Whither?
To nothing dreadful, but to the place from whence thou camest —
to things friendly and akin to thee, to the elements of Being."
— Epictetus

Solitude, as I happen to know from weary experience, has been written about more than enough. Not with the eyes of Argus, the patience of Job, and the years of Methuselah could one hope to read all the tomes, treatises, essays, lyrics, and sonnets composed in its honor. Seers and saints of the Orient have been chanting its praise for three millenniums; ancient misanthropists reviled society in terms of it; in patristic literature it was a perennial theme; more recently, it provided a focal idea of the Romantic Movement. At first thought, then, one might well despair of saying a new word upon a topic so hackneyed and worn; and yet when one burrows into this huge cairn of writing, as I once made it my business to do, one is amazed to find how little fresh thinking it contains and how much mere docile repetition. The newcomer may be encouraged also to discover how few of those who have piled this cairn ever experienced, keenly and at firsthand, the kind of life they praise. I write of what I know.

How does it feel to be living alone, let us say in a cabin among the New England hills? The question has enduring interest, partly because loneliness of some sort is the lot of every human soul, and only a few ever learn to embrace it. Some curiosity, often mingled with a humorous compassion, the world has always shown about those who withdraw from it, vaguely guessing at their motives and rewards, but very seldom does anyone try to discover these rewards and motives

The Cabin Down the Glen

for himself. At most, that is a thing we should like to do if we had the time, the place, and perhaps the courage. Such timid experiments as we sometimes make by camping out or going on lonely walks do not reveal much. They are still expansive, like almost all our activity, and not retractile; they show our western centrifugal tendency and not the centripetal effort of the East; in the language of logic, they are discursive rather than intuitive; and so they differ not only in degree but in kind from the experience of living on one's own land for month after month, wakened by the sunrise and drowsed by the dewfall, watching the young leaves come and the old leaves go, with only one's thoughts for company and only the wind in the pine for an answering voice. No; vagrancy is one good thing, of which I am glad to have had my share and toward which even this legless generation feels some faint atavistic stirrings; but solitude is quite another, and about it America knows very little. For solitude means being still.

The charm and strangeness of this way of life was known ages ago, to the Rishis of China, to the Yogis of India, to the eremites of the deserts along the Nile, and also to many European hermits of the mediaeval world. Very often, while I am sitting here in the sunshine by my cabin door, the lives of those lonely men, their ecstasies and agonies, come to mind. The years and meridians cannot keep them from me; for it is multitude that changes and estranges man from man, but earth and sky and water and fire are ever the same. The voice of the silence has the same low song for me that it sang to Buddha beneath his bo tree. My teachers and guides and companions are such as these: Thoreau in his hut at Walden, William Law at King's Cliffe, Montaigne in his tower at Perigueux, Petrarch at Vaucluse, Raimon Lull in his cell on Majorca, St. Francis on Mount Alverno, Marcus Aurelius on the imperial throne. Very clearly I see the dimmest and farthest away of them all: Lao-Tsze, as he sits astride his mule before the gate opening upon the mountain pass of Han-ku, looking back with a gentle but half-scornful smile at the royal palace of Chow, wherein for many years he has been librarian and professional writer.

Living Alone

Now he has put away those childish things, the world having grown too noisy for a wise man to endure. But while he is waiting there the gatekeeper says to him, knowing his purpose: "I beg you to write a book for me before you go away out of sight;" and Lao-Tsze dismounts, although he well knows that there are already by far too many books in the world — for the date is only six hundred years before Christ — and he writes the five thousand characters of his profoundly simple *Tao Te Ching,* one of the most reverberating books in the world. Then he straddles his white mule again and rides away into the hills of home, and no man knows when or where he died. "When things have displayed their luxuriant growth," he said, "we see them return to their roots. This returning to the root is what we call the state of stillness; and that stillness is a proof that one has fulfilled his appointed end."

Ah, yes, I have companions, by thousands and tens of thousands. It was calculated in the time when Alexandria was almost as soul-withering as our own New York now is that those who had fled from her to live alone in the desert were as many as those who remained behind. India has never been without at least a million hermits. China and Japan and Tibet have always had their lonely "men of the mountains." Wherever in the human past there has been intensest thought or loftiest spiritual aspiration, there, we may be sure, solitude of some kind has also been. The marks of it are unmistakable. A single page of writing, a glimpse of a face, sometimes the mere tones of a voice, will tell me: "This mind has been alone." Not often, to be sure, do we meet such minds in our day, but I refuse to admit on that account that I am doing here either an unique or even an eccentric thing. Rather, it is a perfectly normal thing, as necessary and natural as sleeping, which merely happens just now to be out of fashion. Well, we have seen fashions change. In the meantime, I will not be imprisoned in one epoch or even in one hemisphere, and so I am giving due emphasis to a mode of human experience which America, to her great loss, has hitherto forgotten or ignored.

Deeply significant, whether true to the facts or not, is the

31

The Cabin Down the Glen

alleged discovery of Frobenius that the typical symbol of all races moving westward has been the Altar of the Raying Roads, and that the corresponding symbol of eastward-moving races is the Cavern. But the individual who rounds out and fulfills his life must move both west- and eastward; he must explore the roads of the world and also grope in the cavern of thought; he must look both outward and inward, if only so that he may at last transcend both directions and look upward to our only rest and goal. Just now, as it happens, after wandering along many an outward road, I have come to the mouth of the cavern. And although I am well aware that this is not the final stage, I know also that it is, to me at least, a necessary one. Here I am to learn, like Faust, "im innern ist ein Universum auch."

The business of most solitaries has been nothing less, to use their own great name for it, than the Contemplation of God. But one can no longer employ that phrase with any hope of having it widely understood. To the deeper minds of the Ages of Faith it meant the highest human activity and happiness. To must of us it suggests either laziness or else nonsense. True solitude, at the end of all analysis, is what Plotinus meant by "a flight of the alone to the Alone"; but this too suggests so little in modern ears that one is forced back upon the attempt to define the thing in terms of its accidents rather than its essence. Very well; I accept the hard conditions, and I shall do what I can in spite of them to suggest what solitude is to an American hermit of the twentieth century.

What follows shall not be a panegyric, however, like Peter Damien's or Petrarch's or Rousseau's. These enthusiasts protest so much that I sometimes doubt whether they really enjoyed their lonely living after all, and I often suspect that their underlying and unconscious purpose was not so much to celebrate the eremitic life as it was to make wry faces at society through the loopholes of retreat. That is not my purpose or at all my mood, for if there is anything that I enjoy as I do

Living Alone

solitude, it is the society of my friends and fellows. These are both good things. They answer two alternating needs of human nature. A wise man will use them both intensely, joyously, and with his might.

Solitude is not good for anybody at all times, and indeed I doubt whether it is good for all of us at any time. Obviously, it thrusts the mind inward upon its own resources — and then the mind's only salvation is to have some. When the hermit is "at a loose end," there is no such thing as dropping in on his nearest crony, who is at least forty miles away; or of calling him on the nearest telephone, which should be at least a mile off; or even of turning on the radio, for hermits do not have such things. No; he must simply continue the endless soliloquy: "Says I to myself, says I." For the quality of this entertainment, in which the two lobes of the brain converse together, he is himself solely responsible, and he knows whom to congratulate when it is absorbing. "Doctor Johnson," said the impertinent young Boswell, "please tell me why you talk so much to yourself." "Certainly, Sir," replied the Great Bear. "It is because I like, occasionally, to have an intelligent listener. And also I like to hear what such an intelligent man has to say."

My implication that the discourse of the modern hermit is confined to soliloquy will indicate, to all who have ever thought deeply on these matters, that I am myself a faithless modern, and therefore quite incapacious of the higher solitude. Of course that may be so. Certainly I have come into the woods with an equipment of solid and unquestionable beliefs far slighter than that of my great predecessors, and so perhaps I am lonelier here than they would have been. If I were an ancient pagan, these hills would be the abode of gods; the brook at my doorway would sing me the song and hide from me the wild bright breast of the local nymph; every hemlock would have its dryad and every boulder its gnome. If I were even a mediaeval Christian hermit, one of those heroic souls like Saint Veranus of Vaucluse or Guthlac of Crowland, who went forth against the legions of hell, I should have devils about me in God's plenty — hostile indeed, yet highly conversable. But as it is, what have I?

The Cabin Down the Glen

For me no nymph sings from the upland wood
Her antique song; nor in bright hurrying brook
Is seen, and lost, her sweet elusive smile.

Gone are the maids who ran the ordered race
Or stopped to bathe them by Actaeon's rill,
Narcissus brooding o'er his own fair face,
And Echo laughing from the distant hill.

Under such circumstances solitude may become a more
daunting thing than it once was, and the modern hermit may
often feel not merely alone but lonely. Here, in fact, may be one
of the reasons why so few of us dare to live alone: It has come
to mean not a change of communion, and a change from lower
to higher, but a privation of it. And I think this is likely to hold
with special force in America, where we have so few signs of
any human past. My thoughts go back to the beautiful Valley
of the Seven Kings in the Downs of southern England, and
I feel how warm and friendly would be the companionship of
those royal men who have been sleeping there are least four
thousand years; or I think with envy of Saint Cyprian who
made his hermitage, somewhat ostentatiously, in a ruined
temple of Venus. In my part of Connecticut there is no record
or relic even of Indian occupation, so that I cannot imagine
the Red Men about me or converse with their taciturn ghosts.
On these acres no man has ever lived before me. They have no
place in legend, no genius, no sacred bard. All their warmth of
human meaning is what I give them, and I sometimes feel that
I have hardly enough to go round. There is, in fact, something
humorously pathetic in my effort to make the wild thrushes sing
a human song, to find companions in squirrels and chipmunks
and spiders. This is what prisoners do, not men who have been
enlarged and liberated. I confess it as a fault.

And yet I will not be too humble. If my time and land has
been able to provide me with only a dispeopled earth and,
O, an empty sky! — is the responsibility mine? The utmost that
justice can exact of me is that, like a man born blind, I shall

Living Alone

still strive to see, or never, at any rate, deny the actuality of vision because I have it not. And I will say for myself that little by little the darkness brightens, the silence begins to sing. At least I know, now, that it is a darkness, and that is much to know. When I said, above, that the modern hermit is confined to soliloquy, I was merely being cautious. There may be more, much more for him to hear. This is what I am trying to make sure about: Does any other voice break through? Sometimes that agonizing sense of utter loneliness called solipsism comes over me with such power that I cannot conceive the possibility of any real existence other than that of my own thought, and all the outer universe appears to be my creation. It is in my mind alone, I say, that these birds sing and these clouds float. Such is the terror of solitude. And it has a horror too, when all nature seems to turn suddenly hostile and malign, as it did when Adam and Eve were thrust from the Garden. There are times when I can see nothing but the random and meaningless cruelty of life and when, for God's own sake, I refuse to believe in him. But then — but then there comes a dawn in May, some golden evening in October, or perhaps a breathing midnight full of stars, when every swinging bough makes a divine gesture and every breath of the wind intones a solemn word.

There is, of course, a multitudinous and deeply impressive testimony, swelling up out of all past time, that one who lives alone with Nature is taught by her, however it may be conveyed and whatever its ultimate source, a kind of wisdom that society can never teach. This is the faith behind Bryant's familiar lines:

> To him who in the love of nature holds
> Communion with her visible forms, she speaks
> A various language.

A little way on the other side of Bryant we encounter the

The Cabin Down the Glen

ancient and once universal belief that Nature teaches thus as the spokesman of the Divine. The certainty that "man in the bush with God may meet," and perhaps only there, is almost as old as human thought. It underlies the trust of simple people everywhere in their medicine men, magicians, seers, saints, prophets, lawgivers, poets, and heroes. These, they say, have talked face to face with the gods — for how else is their quite exceptional knowledge or skill or strength, different in kind and not based upon laborious thought or painful experience, to be explained? And the gods, it is generally agreed, dwell by preference in the wilderness, ignoring the cages of wood and stone that men construct for their imprisonment. One must go forth to find them.

Only in terms of this ancient faith, now nearly forgotten, can we understand the numerous cognate legends, such as that of Jehovah giving the Ten Commandments to Moses on the wild summit of Sinai and of the nymph Egeria in her sacred grove dictating to Numa Pompilius the laws of Rome. It helps us to comprehend the oracles of Apollo and of Ge, the earth goddess, all in wild places, as well as the effort of musicians and soothsayers to translate the vague messages of Zeus as whispered by the sacred oak of Dodona. Supreme spiritual insight and elevation were anciently thought to come only to the man who waits alone in silence, as the legends of the Buddha, Jesus, Mohammed, and Saint Francis remind us. Poets were supposed, as Horace said, to "love the groves and to flee from the city," and this for no fanciful reason but because the Muses upon whom they were wholly dependent would meet them only in the wilderness. It was while Hesiod was shepherding his lambs, walking alone in the mist under holy Helicon, that the daughters of Zeus taught him glorious song.

The examples of this belief are indeed innumerable, and they reach from the dawn of intellectual time far down into the nineteenth century. When the philosophers from the imperial court asked Saint Anthony, father of Christian hermits, how he, who had never learned to read or write and had lived alone for fifty years in the desert, could yet dispute so ably on the

Living Alone

highest and subtlest themes, he replied: "I have been taught by the book of Nature." Saint Bernard of Clairvaux, one of the most learned men of the mediaeval world, declared that he had won all his erudition from the oaks and beeches. He wrote to a young disciple: "Take it from one who knows, that you will find more wisdom in the forest than in books. Wood and stone will teach you things not to be had from human masters." To that remark Wordsworth adds nothing whatever in the stanza, so much misunderstood and ridiculed:

> *One impulse from a vernal wood*
> *Will teach you more of man,*
> *Of moral evil and of good,*
> *Than all the sages can.*

Is this mere nonsense, unworthy of attention in our enlightened times, a fragment of intellectual history showing how men thought before they attained our intelligence? For my part, I have too deep a veneration for many who thought thus and too strong a respect for the intuitive wisdom of the untold thoughtless millions to say so. This faith is now dead, but that does not prove it false. Argument did not kill it, but the simple substitution of another faith — in science. We were taught that we should no longer need it. Well, I find that I do. It was the religious groundwork of all triumphant solitude. The loss of it has tended greatly to impoverish our modern world, leaving us shallow and guideless and lonely.

In its origin, perhaps the belief that Nature speaks to the spirit of the solitary man was connected with "animism," but during historic ages it has usually assumed the presence in nature of supernatural powers with whom man may learn to commune. Faith in these powers was refined and elevated during the ages without being lost, for Wordsworth still invokes it when he speaks of

> *a sense sublime*
> *Of something far more deeply interfused,*

The Cabin Down the Glen

Whose dwelling is the light of setting suns
And the round ocean and the living air,
And the blue sky, and in the heart of man.

It is etherealized still further, but without essential change, in Emerson's phrase "Nature is the symbol of the spirit" and in his assertion that she is merely "a discipline of the understanding in spiritual truths." Wordsworth and Emerson held fast all their lives to this belief, but the man who taught them much of what they knew lost it in mid-career — and so ceased to be a poet. Taken with all its implications, one of the most piercing cries in literature is that of Coleridge:

O Lady! we receive but what we give,
And in ourselves alone doth Nature live.

I never read those heartbreaking words without seeing the old religions crumble, the old sanctities fade, and the skies of all the older poetry come ruining down. It is very like the cry that once shuddered across the Mediterranean: "Great Pan is dead!" Then and there began a spiritual solitude such as the hermits of old days never had to endure. For we have found nothing that fills the void thus left — no religion relating us anew to the Infinite, no sense of holy awe, no poetry or other art that even strives in the grand old way to be *magister vitae* [director/teacher of life]. The nature that was once a common abode of gods and men, our familiar home, sounding with voices of stern or tender admonishment, has become a meaningless medley of atoms from which the mind shrinks back aghast. We are told that the world depicted by science is every day more wonderful. In fact, it is every day more bewildering. Speaking in human terms, which are ultimately all that matter, it grows continually more incredible, crushing and alien to the human heart.

❧

Living Alone

Perhaps because I have come too late into the world, I cannot revive in myself the ancient faith that Nature is God's mouthpiece. Another reason may be that I know too much about her, having seen her do things that Wordsworth and Emerson either did not see or else were able to ignore. Or, finally, it may be that I expect too much of God. In any case, I agree with Socrates rather than with Saint Bernard in feeling that the trees have little to teach me which I do not already know. The hermitage is indeed an admirable seed plot for ideas and perhaps even wisdom, but the seeds themselves must be brought from society, and the plants, if they are ever to mature, must grow up there.

Neither, so far as I can see, is there a sufficient moral and intellectual discipline in living alone. One must be strong when he begins it, for the lax and inert hermit is certain first to lean and then to fall toward that side to which he is naturally inclined.

Most of us are like trees that have grown in a dense forest, needing the shade and shelter and support of our fellows. But in solitude we have to stand alone, like the single tree round which the forest has been felled. This is what I mean in saying that some cannot endure solitude. Only here and there is one who can; but he who can, should. He is like the great jack pine carefully chosen by the lumber men of the Maine woods to fight the north wind singly and to replenish half a township.

And yet it would be easy to exaggerate the loneliness of even a modern solitude, and I have no wish to do so. On the contrary, I would record, as one of the major gains I have made here, a new and thrilling sense of society, of our incalculable debt to the human past and of our mutual dependence. Strange and paradoxical it may be that one should have to wrench himself free from men in order to realize for the first time clearly how he is forever bound to mankind, but so it has been with me. The more I have striven toward independence, the more I have felt supported, and every effort toward a deeper seclusion has merely increased my awareness of the innumerable human multitude.

The Cabin Down the Glen

Ever since the time of Rousseau, and indeed for at least two thousand years before that, there has been in the western world a primitivistic dream, always bound to recur in aging civilizations, which extols the ignorance of the so-called "happy savage" and aspires to imitate him, abandoning all the wealth of civilization. I have no such illusions about savage life and no intention of such abandonment, even supposing that it were now possible. It is true that I have given up most of the trinkets and bric-a-brac and noisy gadgets of the contemporary world. These, however, are the products not of civilization but of barbarism, and the very absence of them enables me to realize how precious are the few things, all old and indispensable, that I have brought with me into the woods.

I find a sort of happiness in naming these, in counting our human treasure, almost every item in which has been won by ages of toil with hand or wit. Take first these seeds of fire, sleeping until I wake them. Our control of the power that lies hidden in such bits of red phosphorus has made one of the major differences between us and the beasts, or something so nearly bestial that only an anthropologist would quarrel about the distinction. Consider these seeds of the edible grasses, wheat and rye and barley and oats, that I sift through my fingers. Do you know that they are also the seeds, in a sense hardly metaphorical, of cities also, and of all that cities have meant to us? — For before we found or invented them we could live only as hunters, few, weak, savage, and miserable. To whom do we owe them? To the nameless myriads of a past with no other record. All we can say is that wherever civilization first shows itself these are found. And who first discovered that by mixing a fungus with edible grains they could make bread and beer? Thousands of men and women; and I am in debt to them all. So I am to other thousands who invented the wheel, and to the millions who developed the knife, the hoe, the axe, the scythe, the saw, and hammer and nails. For we moderns, wonderful though we may be, did not make these things, nor could we. Far nearer the truth it would be to say that they made us; and we should show ourselves more intelligent as well as more grateful

Living Alone

if we did not take them quite so serenely for granted. Nor must I forget the many skills and crafts, the intricate and delicate ways of shaping things to our human needs, each of them old beyond computation, that have been brought together in my small cabin. Under this roof and within these walls that defend me from wind and rain I have a table, a bed, a chair, lamp and candles, window and door, hearth and chimney — every one a pure gift from the laborious human past. Is this independence? Is this "going back to Nature"? Is this really living alone?

Let me name now a few treasures of the mind, all social in origin, that I have brought with me. Glancing at my bookshelf, I see that I have the Bible and Homer and Virgil, Seneca and Horace, Petrarch and Boccaccio and Leopardi, Ronsard and Theophile de Viau, Milton, Thomson, Cowper, Alfred de Vigny, Victor de Laprade, Lamartine, Wordsworth and Byron and Meredith, Moody and Abercrombie and Carman and Frost. So much for poets. In prose I have much of Rousseau, Zimmerman's enormous *Einsamkeit* — in the first, four-volume edition — Petrarch's Latin letters, Emerson and Thoreau. Is this solitude, or is it a society? At one side of the cabin stands a tiny piano, and on it are all of Beethoven's and Mozart's sonatas, nearly everything that Brahms wrote for this instrument, and oceanic quantities of Bach. Is this what is meant by living alone? The hermit thrushes will not have it so, for when I begin to play they come out of the depths of the wood and sing on the nearest boughs.

In a still higher rank among the precious things that bind me to my fellows, I must mention language — a gift so wonderful that many sober men have thought it must come not from humanity at all but from the gods. Even here, where it might seem least useful, language is perhaps the best thing society has given me. Though I should meet no other human being in a month, and though I should read no book and write no line, still it would serve me in many indispensable ways. Consider the companionship that language maintains between mind and mind apparently separated by seas and ages, and the assurance it brings into every hour that millions of others have toiled and

The Cabin Down the Glen

wrought and hoped and failed as we do. It is in solitude that I have the fullest realization of this communion. My sense of our fellowship, as we huddle here on our lonely planet, is never stronger than when I am alone, perhaps under the stars at night, when there drifts into mind some phrase from the sea of the human past: "Sunt lacrimae rerum, et mentem mortalia tangunt," [Here too there are tears for things (i.e., the affairs of life), and the conditions of mortals touch the mind/heart.] or "When to the sessions of sweet silent thought I summon up remembrance," or "The Lord is my shepherd; I shall not want," or "Uber allen Gipfeln ist Ruh." [There is rest/peace over all the tree-tops.] But it need not be a famous phrase, or a phrase of any kind. Many a single word, tossed up into consciousness, worn and beautiful with immemorial use and still warm from the beating of human hearts, can charm away all loneliness.

It is to language, moreover, that I owe at least a good half of "this intellectual being, these thoughts that wander through eternity." I know very well how it paralyzes thought and stiffens it into ossified phrases, and I know the lifelong struggle to master language without being mastered by it; I have often been angry with words for their stubbornness and disgusted by their blunt refusals; but just now, trying to fancy what my life would be without this guide and mentor, how drifting and shapeless as the mist of the river, how idle and purposeless, I give my deepest thanks for the treasure of speech. It builds a stockade round the mind, staving off the wilderness, shutting out chaos. I came to this place to think, and language is my tool as certainly as axe and saw and hammer were used to build my cabin. I did not make it, nor could I. Rather, it has made me. Mankind has made it, working altogether through all time, and in everything that I think or say the total human voice is stronger than my own.

And mankind has worked at this supreme task in a very mysterious way. No single worker has ever foreseen the total fabric of any language. Each has striven merely to serve his temporary need. And yet what a marvel has been wrought! If we wished to impress a visitor from Mars, we could do nothing better than to show him the precision and the subtle

Living Alone

symmetrical beauty of the Greek verb — except that after seeing that masterpiece he would expect better things of us than we could now perform. How was this beautiful strong thing fashioned? As though a multitude of blind men should take to throwing stones — and so build the Parthenon! Every delicate device of language has been produced in the same strange, purposeless, and wholly social way. No hermit, no pedant, and certainly no grammarian has ever added the least appreciable increment to its powers. It has been made by the fumbling and unintentional but wholly miraculous art of Everyman. It is the gift of all to each. Oh, the best thing that Crusoe saved from his shipwreck was not powder and shot, not hammer and nails, not his Bible even, but language. If I were in his situation, my most besetting fear would be lest this treasure might gradually sift and melt away from memory, and I should spend an hour of every day in writing on the sand or talking to the palm trees, as he did to his parrot, so as to maintain my citizenship in the ordered world of words, of thoughts, and of men.

For so long as one has ordered words, thoughts cling to them, and men are never far away. It is to language in great part that we owe the logical frames or patterns of our thinking, its very shapes and channels; and, although I am trying to work free from some of these, to abandon all would mean sheer insanity. Alone am I? And have I really, in the stupid jargon of the time, "returned to Nature"? On the contrary. The farther I get from the meaningless contemporary noises, the more I can think; and the more I think, the closer I come to all mankind, and especially to those of the great society. I think with the minds of other men, most of whom have been long "dead," — although just what it would mean to be "alive" if these are not, I am unable to guess. The country of my mind is threaded from horizon to horizon by the paths they have worn there. Up this darkling hill goes Jesus; Virgil and Dante tread that plunging vale; through the thicket yonder strays Thoreau; and Plato stands on the heights. Or, to put it in another way: when I am sitting alone in the sunshine by my cabin door, far from any human sound or sight, then really, in

The Cabin Down the Glen

no metaphorical and certainly in no boastful sense but in the simplest, I am least alone. *Numquam minus solus quam solus* [I am never less alone than when alone.], as Scipio said long ago while sitting in the sunshine by his cabin door at Linternum. For it is then that I cease to be an individual, at least in the narrow way of one engaged in conflict or debate. I become a person, or, as it were, a society, unlimited by race, epoch, clime, religion, manners, and the like — a society including Orient and Occident, ancient and modern and mediaeval, rich and poor, subtle and simple, learned and ignorant, wise and foolish, virtuous and vicious, humble and great. Having no appearances to keep up, no social ladder to climb, and no axe to grind except an actual one, I can afford to be hospitable. No one is turned from my door. That golden pool of sunshine under the maple boughs, where the bee hums in the bracken and the guttural brook glides by, is really a populous place while I am sitting there, alone, in the afternoon. Lao-Tsze meets Walt Whitman there and finds many things in common. Thoreau finds that nearly all he ever said had been said two thousand years before him by the Cynics of ancient Greece. St. Francis answers Voltaire, Henry More confutes John Locke, and Shelley agrees with Spinoza. Oh, what a world of good talk! As for me, a good part of the time I give to "thought" is really spent in listening.

I once had a dear friend, gone now, with whom I used to sit by the fireside for hour after happy hour with hardly a word spoken. On our walks in the Connecticut woods, in the Adirondacks, and in the English Cotswolds, it was chiefly in silence that we conversed. Well, I have him still. The quiet of this place is the same as that in which we used to meet, and it gives him back to me. Bliss Carman is with me by this fireside, which he never saw. He walks with me under these hemlocks, which he would have loved as I do. I never see the stars come out above my eastern hill without hearing again that most musical and eloquent silence that has ever vibrated between me and any living man.

By this time, it should be clear that my solitude is not a rejection of any good thing. I have not come here because

Living Alone

I have had too much of society but because I have had too little. I am not going "back to Nature" but lifting her along with me. This is not a retreat but an advance. Although I love Nature and the past as much as it is good for any man to do, I do not wish to go backward in any sense. Our human way is onward, forever; and this means to me, among other things, that we should be ever more and more human, more civilized, more deeply and fully social.

If it were not for sullying these pages with what might look like a hatred born of fear and suffering, and if it were not for the pain it costs me to remember how millions of my fellowmen spend their few brief years, I might draw a picture now that would bring into vivid relief the kind of life I lead and would give some clue to my motives. Not in a mood of complacency or of self-congratulation but in that of pity, rather, I might speak of those aimless and bewildered multitudes, among whom are not a few men and women that I love, who have never known quietness, have never heard the song of silence, have never ·experienced the joy of a steady inward growth. They toil at they know not what, seldom even daring to ask whether their work has any human worth or whether it be not positively baneful. They toil they know not why, but chiefly in order to "keep up appearances" — in the eyes of fools. Lost and disheartened in a world that is visibly going to pieces, they toil on, when they are allowed to, tinkering at the old machine, spending their strength and skill and the wealth of the spirit in threshing the wind, and taking chaff in return. What wonder that they go mad in steadily growing numbers, so that every increase in "civilization" brings a corresponding increase of insane asylums, or that they blow out their brains, or lapse into all manner of bestiality? It is rather their patient endurance of the slow tragedy of modern life that should make a wise man marvel, and that almost breaks the heart.

And see by whom they are led! As William Vaughn Moody

The Cabin Down the Glen

saw years ago, "They were better captainless." For the captains can think of only this terrible thing to say: "Let us run still faster, toil even more furiously, and toss our children with a stronger frenzy into the furnaces of Moloch — and all will soon be well." In a sense, this is probably so, for the final crash and ruin of the Western world may be thereby somewhat accelerated. Meanwhile, the simple and no longer escapable fact is that we have built our wonderful house upon the sands, and that a great voice is just now becoming distinctly audible, saying: "Thou fool, this night thy soul shall be required of thee!"

At such a time in the world's affairs, what can a man do to help — a man who feels as I feel it his incalculable debt and obligation to mankind? Shall he add his voice to the shouters? Shall he too rush here and there? Shall he get himself elected, or wealthy, or famous, so that he may increase his "influence?" Or might he do perhaps as well if he should strive not so much to do as to be something, since this at least is rarer and has not been so much tried in our day? Perhaps, now that all his fellows are giving their lives to action, with results that leave much to be desired, he might set forth upon the ancient adventure of thought. Now that the stupid boasters of prosperity have had their mouths stopped for a time, he might say a quiet word about inward wealth. But better and more persuasive than anything he could say would be the example of a life lived quietly with the First Things, a life resting down upon the things found true, a life delving under and soaring over the wreck of the present to the things that everlastingly endure.

Must I pause here to meet the charge of selfishness, sure to be brought in a time like ours against a way of life like mine? The doctrine of "social service," never criticized, everywhere ignorantly bandied about, grossly misinterpreted to mean meddling in our neighbors' business and corresponding neglect of our own, is still a potent shibboleth among us, and with the poisonous results of it Christendom is sick unto death. We have

Living Alone

reached such a nadir of stupidity with regard to this problem of "service" and "selfishness" that the man who spends all his time in collecting dollars or in improving his game of golf or in trying to impose his notions of private morality upon his fellows is considered a "public servant," while the man who spends a few months in the effort to relate himself to the universe is thought a deserter from the ranks. How, then, can I hope to be understood?

Well, I deny, in the first place, that the question "How shall the world be served?" is ever a primary question, at least in time. Is it not obvious enough, even yet, that the service can never be better than the servant? When that becomes quite clear, and when we come to realize that we do not stand so much in need of more activity as we do of more wisdom, then I think we shall see that by a few pauses of preparation such as mine, the world stands ultimately to gain. But now the world is crowded to suffocation with eager enthusiasts all shouting the modern equivalent of "Here am I, Lord! Send me!" The trouble is that when they are sent, they are utterly at a loss where to go. Are these servants? Their zeal for "service" is something, no doubt, but fitness would be something too.

And, in the second place, I seriously believe that our distracted world needs nothing more just now, even in the way of "service," than the spectacle and example of a few persons going serenely about their proper business of plain living and high thinking, unashamed, unhurried, and undismayed. Other needs are perhaps more obvious, certainly more advertised, and yet who can fail to see that the inmost woe of our time, underlying all its superficial anxieties, is just that we have no sense of goal, no assured indefeasible hope, no fundamental faith? When I walk in the streets of the city, as Dante walked in Hell, it is not so much the fear of poverty as the terror of emptiness that I see in the people's eyes. They live in a world without purpose or meaning, without beauty or inward peace, so that the most compassionate observer must ask himself whether it is worth the effort to sustain in them that life for which they see no value. I can often surmise that they once hoped for something better

The Cabin Down the Glen

and that some of them now feel defrauded, but in most of the faces where youth no longer serves as a painted screen, it is plain that hope lies dead. So dead it is that although "social service" may keep these corpses moving for a while longer, may galvanize them into a semblance of activity, may even find them ropes to pull at here and there as the dead bodies are made to do in "The Ancient Mariner" — yet this whole effort seems no more than a disguised cruelty. Only one thing can do them permanent good: They must be born again. Confidence in the total scheme, sense of direction, assurance of Something that endures and that gives a noble meaning to our few days — only this can help them. They must be brought back to the First Things, which are as few and simple and uncostly as the natural elements — fire, earth, water, and air — and just as essential to anything that may rightly be called human life.

What thoughtful and observant person does not know this? And yet who acts upon this knowledge? "There are a thousand persons," as Thoreau says, "who are hacking at the branches of evil to one who is striking at the root." Oh, they have been led by the blind, these blind people of our city streets. For those who should have been their leaders have dragged God out of the skies and have then most dismally failed to find him again in Humanity. They have harried God out of Nature — or so they think — and have been unable to rediscover Him in Science. All this might perhaps have been endured if He had not been driven also from the throne in the heart; but this is, and has long been, an empty throne, and nothing whatever is done to fill it by the frenzied activity of our "social servants" and our "public-minded citizens."

There was once a Servant of Man who prepared himself for speech by thirty years of silence, who taught far more by what he was than by anything he did or said, and who lived a great part of his life alone. He lived near the earth all his days, gaining from it serenity, poise, faith, and the kind of wisdom that sees into the heart of things. He had a handicraft, and it taught him patience, confidence, power. He was always very poor, and he did nothing to enrich either himself or his friends

Living Alone

and family. It was poverty of the spirit alone that concerned him. He was in no sense a reformer, a Puritan, or a moralist. He prohibited nothing. He was not anxious about sin because he tried to lead men into that great light in which sin withers away. He put the First Things first. He said, "Seek ye first the Kingdom of God."

There is nothing new in the doctrine of social service, and the contribution of our time has been chiefly in the way of misinterpretation and vulgarizing. Primitive Christianity gave it an important but strictly subordinate place — and if we had held it in that place, we might be Christian still. Seneca thought out its implications in the palace of Nero as wisely as any man has ever done. Boethius in his prison cell saw its true bearings more clearly than we do. The holier monks and hermits of the Middle Ages — yes, precisely those men against whom, since the days of Luther, we have ignorantly brought the charge of "selfishness" — never forgot it by day or night, but were constantly concerned, as we should be, with the question of how the world is to be served most effectively, whether by the active or by the contemplative life. They served in both of these ways, as we should, but the upshot of their thousand years of thinking and their thousand books of writing on the problem was that the higher service is rendered by the labor not of the hand but of the mind and spirit, or, in other words, that Being is ultimately more helpful than Doing.

For the destruction of this high doctrine we have to thank Martin Luther, the runagate monk who failed egregiously at his task of inward labor but succeeded in external activity like a storm-wind. No fool in the ways of this world, however foolish he may have been in those of all that surrounds it, he knew where to begin; and one of the first things he laid his thick hands upon was the doctrine and tradition of religious leisure, the Contemplatio Dei. This, said he, arguing from his own incompetence, is mere selfish laziness; and millions who were equally incapable and equally jealous of all excellence they could not share, echoed his voice. Thus we turned away from God toward our own sick selves. Thus the modern world, which

The Cabin Down the Glen

might have had the heaven of heavens for its dwelling place, has turned, like Faust at the end of all his struggle, to digging ditches. Martin Luther is the shadowy President who sits, ex officio, on most of our Committees. Martin Luther is the father of modern business, and John Calvin is its uncle.

In some ways, of course, taking the long view of history, it may have been a good thing that human energy was thus furiously concentrated for a time upon activity and the physical world, so that the work to be done there might be as soon as possible completed. On our long westward march from Punjab to the Pacific we were already, when Luther spoke, nearing the last and the most exhausting lap — America. He lightened our burden and sped us on the way by telling us not to ask why or whither we were marching, but to march. Very well; we have obeyed him. We have arrived at the end of the distance he pointed toward; and behold, it is not very good. If this that we see about us were all, we might far better not have come. But is this necessarily the end? May it not rather be the beginning?

With less than the proverbial half-an-eye one can see that the army of westward marchers, with its banner of the Raying Roads, is now slowly stumbling to a stand. Just ahead yawns the mouth of the Cavern. In other words, the energy we have been pouring forth for a hundred barbarous generations in the conquest of nature and of each other must soon be drawn inward, for the conquest of ourselves and the search after what is higher. Leisure of some sort will soon be the portion of all, bringing swift destruction to many and opening new horizons for a few. This will not be our choice but our destiny. It is close upon us, and we are not ready. We have no guides, or prophets even. Church and School give no help. Just where they are most "advanced" they are in fact most reactionary and most recreant, striving to make us believe that all we need for salvation is more and ever more of that same external activity which has brought us so near to death. They cannot even see that millions of us are at this moment facing the frontiers of mind and spirit for the first time, with no more courage and skill

50

Living Alone

for the adventure than they could learn by the tide-waters of prosperity, while living in fat content. O for a few Daniel Boones and Kit Carsons to blaze the trails of this new Wild West! O for some modern John the Baptist to cry out "Simplify! Simplify!" on the edge of this new wilderness!

One such pioneer we have had, but he came and went too soon for an American following. Nietzsche and Max Stirner could find him in Germany, W.H. Hudson in the Argentine, Unamuno in Spain, and Mahatma Ghandi in India, where he is not needed, but we who need Henry David Thoreau most of all have as yet no conception of his inner meaning. Do we not still regard him as a naturalist, a wild man, a misanthropic hermit? Except most superficially, he was none of these. Thoreau was a pathfinder in the spiritual hinterland. To his generation he said, as he would say even more sternly to ours: "Your way runs inward." No other American, not even Emerson himself, has ever seen and said so clearly that man does not live by bread alone. His daily life, beautifully bare and simple, drove that doctrine home.

Considering all this, and remembering what a tower of strength the example of Thoreau has long been to me, I can never read without a pang that brief passage in which he grazes the problem of service. "I must confess," he says, "that I have felt mean enough when asked how I was to act on society, what errand I had to mankind. Undoubtedly I did not feel mean without reason, and yet my loitering is not without defense. I would fain communicate the wealth of my life to men, would really give them what is most precious in my gift... I enclose and foster the pearl till it is grown. I wish to communicate those parts of my life which I would gladly live again myself."

Now it is understandable enough that a brisk worldling such as Robert Louis Stevenson should call Thoreau "a skulker" — and also that he should take back this epithet when he was misinformed about Thoreau's activities on the "Underground Railroad." But must we believe that Thoreau himself made this mistake, even for a moment? Was he also overborne at times by the doubts that assail every man who stands alone? Was it

The Cabin Down the Glen

sometimes almost a greater loneliness than even he could bear to see all America racing headlong in the opposite direction? Why not? For we have to consider that he could have run fast and far in that same direction if he had not found something better to do. What an admirable engineer, what a road maker and bridge builder and forest queller and mountain tunneller was lost to America when he sat down in Concord to make notes in his Journal! With that keen, shrewd Yankee wit of his, what a fortune he might have amassed! Instead, he took day wages for about three months of the year and did "nothing" for the rest of the time. When most of his footloose neighbors rushed off to the California gold fields, he sat by his woodland pond, thinking. For in spite of all momentary doubts, he knew where his true wealth lay and that a stream from the mountains of gold came down through his native valley. He did his work in part by a wise and somewhat conspicuous abstention from the work of others, and also by continually asking what work should be done, and why. The President at Washington was not doing anything more serviceable. He exemplified the truth of that noble line in which John Milton towered up for a moment above his own over-anxious Puritanism: "They also serve who only stand and wait." And I think there must have come to him many a quiet hour of assurance in which he knew that the utmost we can do to lighten the world's care is to attain serenity for ourselves and then to radiate it, that the best consolation we can bring to the sorrow of the world is brought by our happiness, and that the most effective answer to noise is simply to be still.

"A man does not seek to see himself," says Chuang Tsu, "in a running stream." Only that which is still in itself can reflect stillness upon others." And again he says: "When water is still, it is a perfect Level, and the greatest artificer takes his rule from it."

ॐ

Living Alone

But now once more, what is the essential quality and nature of this living alone? How shall I name or describe it, if not in the great language that Thomas Aquinas took from Aristotle, or in the noble phrase of Plotinus? Well, at least I can say what it is not. My delight in the shows and sounds of earth and sky is not the central thing, for this I had in my wandering days as keenly as I have it now. The thoughts of poets and musicians, although they take on a new grandeur from these surroundings, do not fill my time or mind. I have just been reading Virgil, for example, and have found that he is not to be understood in a library. But I did not come here to read, and I perfectly understand what Emerson meant in saying that books are for the scholar's idle hours. Even that sense of great human companionship of which I have spoken, although it is certainly one of the best of my rewards, is not what I find, or surmise, at the very heart of solitude.

Pure and essential solitude as I know it is a rare experience, not to be attained at once merely by providing the outward conditions. A man may shut himself away from his fellows for months at a time and never have this experience — or, again, it may come to him at noonday on Fifth Avenue. It is hard to describe, partly because the description must be made in a mood that is alien to it. With me it seems to begin with an unusual quiet of body and mind, when I desire nothing, regret nothing, and think nothing. The concentration of ordinary thought is dispersed. I become like the crow on the treetop, seeing everything because his eye is focused nowhere. Inner and outer, self and not-self, passive and active seem to merge. It is as though my thought were emptying in order to be filled. And then comes an inward glow and warmth, an assurance, a resting down and a surrender to something greater than I am, greater than any man, greater than all men, a shelter from the storms of time, a rock in a weary land. I suppose that the whole experience is essentially religious and mystical.

As the days and the weeks wheel over I grow more intent — that is to say, stretched inward. The outer world of events and persons dwindles and the intellectual world of history and

The Cabin Down the Glen

thought and art sinks down until I see it far away. It is not that I lose interest in them but rather that I seem to be looking through them at what they mean. Their interest is enhanced, indeed, by the increasing distance, like that of mountains on the skyline. They are time's children, and beautiful with the pathos of time, but all their reality is reflected from elsewhere as the light of the moon from the sun. They are bathed in a glory not theirs. They are listening to a song. The stars listen, and the quiet hills about me, and all the hemlocks and ferns of the glen when the wind is hushed. My old shadowy companions are listening, and I listen with them, to a deep everlasting song that comes from the farther shore of silence.

In speaking of that song I fear that I shall seem to talk sheer nonsense, and yet speak of it I must because it is sung by the voice of solitude. Need I say that I know almost nothing about it, except as bare experience? I do not even know whether it is in fact a song or a silence. I only know its power upon me and its increasing hold. The thoughts and moods that come and go, my own or those of other men, are no interruption, for it sounds from beyond thought, as something simpler and more necessary. It dims the beloved landscape and mutes all other voices. It seems to be drawing me little by little away from space and time, out of the glitter and the glow, up from the Many toward the One. Although I have gone as yet only a short way, I often seem to be looking back from their sunward side upon earth's creatures, once so dark and solid against the light, and to find them fairer, indeed, than ever before, but less substantial, with a tone of farewell about them in all the air of afternoon. It is as though, having loved them long and passionately for their own sakes, I love them now far more for what they shadow forth.

Living Alone

During the last hour a benediction of deep quiet has lingered in the woods and over my cabin, as though some masterful voice had spoken: "Peace. Be still." No zephyr has whispered under the eaves. No bee has hummed at the window pane. Even the little aspen tree near the window has said no audible word. All sounds of men are shut away behind the miles of forest. Only, at long drowsing intervals, there has drifted to me from far down the glen some silver globe of tone from the song of the hermit thrush — remote, meditative, cool, faintly brushing the fringe of quiet. Elsewhere no sound, no motion, either among the carven ferns of the glen floor, or among the millions of leaves that float on the lake of the air, or aloft in the sky where the sun strides over, "counting his hilltops one by one."

Absolute silence can hardly exist, I know, on our busy hurrying planet, and we must use the word with constant reference to our own powers of perception. If I had the miraculous ears of that old Welsh bard who could hear the grass-blades growing, there would be no silence for me anywhere, and I should now be hearing the trampling hooves of a thousand ants, the spinning-wheel of the spider, the breathing of the beetle, the thunder of uncrumpling ferns, and the roar of the rivers of sap pouring upward to dapple the hemlock. Fortunate it is for me, then, that the intricate physics and chemistry of the forest, all its unimaginable hydraulics and engineering, have been hushed to the sub-audible; for although I delight in many sounds, I am fond of silence too and would not care to have it taken from me.

By many men and women, it would seem, silence is felt to be faintly hostile, vaguely ominous, or perhaps overcharged with expectancy. Otherwise, how to explain their ingenious defenses against it, by means of radio sets and victrolas, mechanical pianos and claxons, rumble of metropolitan traffic, and even talk? Something of the same instinct may be seen among primitive tribes, beating on their tom-toms far into the night to drive off the noisy silences of the jungle. Yet this is by no means a universal feeling. I myself have known deep silences in many

55

The Cabin Down the Glen

places and of many kinds, and almost always, after the first shock of strangeness, I have found them friendly. They have been like the solitary lakes of our western mountains, somewhat daunting at first in their majestic loneliness; but long ago my thoughts learned to step down and bathe in them unafraid.

Silence is the solitude of the ear. It sinks inward, quieting the heart. And just as living alone deepens the sense of society, so this privation of sound makes a rich amends, giving back far more than it takes away. At any rate, that is what I find. I have no means of knowing how common the experience is of hearing an imaginary music, far away, never clamorous, but always immense. The young David heard it during his long nights in the hills with his sheep about him, for it is often echoed in the Psalms; Pythagoras heard it by the Mediterranean and explained it as the "Music of the Spheres"; Emerson may have had it in mind when he wrote Fore-runners; but I have found only one extended description of it — in the Fourteenth Book of Tolstoy's *War and Peace*, where it comes to the boy Petya as he sits in the rain on an army wagon listening to a wonderful music through all the hours of darkness on the night before his death. But then, Tolstoy knew everything.

Too vague for memory to repeat, too vast for any notation, this music marches on before me or falls from the sky by night and by day. I do not recall it as music heard in the past, nor do I improvise it in the present. I am passive to it. I merely overhear. My thoughts may turn away for hours or days, but when I listen again it is there, sounding on and on, never loud but always voluminous and inexhaustibly strong, like the surge and clangor of a sea beach far away. Sometimes I think that I have wandered near the ocean of sound that Bach and Beethoven knew, that sea from which they dipped their tiny thimblefuls of tone.

જ⊷

And beyond even this, farther from the senses but closer to the heart, at the deep core of the quiet, there may be some-

Living Alone

thing more. Who am I that I should name it, even? Yet only the night before last, as I was lying beside a haystack on my highest hill, it seemed to name itself. The crescent moon was low in the west, where I could still see some colors of sunset. A few stars were out. An owl was calling. A breeze moved in the leaves overhead. It was one of those magical moments when a man feels in tune not only with the earth and the stars but with whatever great Being it is that sustains them, and when serenity descends upon him, he knows not whence or how. All at once, out of that quietness yet within it too, it was as though a voice were speaking the words of the Psalm: "Be still, and know that I am God." And then came those words from the *Book of Wisdom*: "When all things are in silence and night is in her swift course, thine almighty word, O Lord, leaps down from heaven."

I do not know what these things mean. During the greater part of my life they have meant to me nothing whatever. But I should give an imperfect account of my living alone if I failed to say that I sometimes think I hear a voice in these lonely acres like that heard calling long ago in the Garden: "Adam! Where art thou?"

THE SPRING IN THE MEADOW

The eternal God is thy dwelling-place, and underneath
are the everlasting arms.

— Deuteronomy XXX, 27

The wise will live by faith —
Faith in the order of things, and that this order is sound.
— Robert Bridges,
in *The Testament of Beauty*

When I return to my work on the land after several months
of metropolitan life, I always find that I must learn all over
again the simplest rural occupations. At planting or sowing, at
digging with spade or hoe, at swinging the axe or the scythe,
I work badly and painfully at first, not only because I am
unaccustomed but because I use a wasteful rhythm, acquired
in the city, which does not fit the task. My motions are self-
assertive, as though I had all the work to do alone, without
help, even against a stout resistance. I catch myself thinking
about these wild acres as though they were utterly mine, to
wreak my will upon, to conquer and to rule.

But they seem to have other plans. During the ages before
my advent here they have acquired a bent of character and a
trend of purpose which they will not instantly put off to serve
my whim. They hardly seem to realize that I have been given
divine authority, according to Genesis, to "subdue" them and
to have "dominion" over them. And I confess that I am myself
a good deal puzzled when I read that wise old book to find
that this same subjection to man's will is part of the curse
that Jehovah lays upon Eve: "In pain shalt thou bring forth
children, and thy desire shall be to thy husband, and he shall

The Spring in the Meadow

rule over thee." How can it be in the one case a blessing and in the other a curse? I suspect that it cannot and that it always curses the Adam who exerts it, whether upon Eve or upon the Nature she stands for, as much as Nature and Eve are cursed by it.

To be sure, the law, nearly always an ass, declares these acres "mine." (Until recent decades did it not use a very similar language about a man's wife?) I may spoil them by bending them violently to my will. It has been left in the power of man to rape and ruin the beauty about him, spreading the contagion of his inward ugliness — and this is what, for the most part, on our continent, he has done — but Nature will really respond, like Eve, to nothing less than trustful cooperation, partnership and love. Until I adopt this attitude, I am sent back to my cabin, night after night, worn out in body and spirit, discouraged, and beaten.

In those first days I often pause a moment to glance up at the huge white pine that overlooks the scene of my labors. He has been there since before the Revolutionary War, whereas I have arrived quite recently, and so it is presumable that he knows more about the customs of the place than I do; and yet, rather absurdly, I find myself at first regarding him as the intruder. I resent his serenity. There is an unspoken rebuke in the quietness with which he looks down upon me, as though he were quoting Emerson: "Why so hot, little Sir?" But then I begin to wonder how it is that he succeeds with such apparent ease while I am always failing. I ask myself whether it is because, in the hundred and fifty winters that he has been facing the storm wind, he has learned to take what comes, and because, in the still nights of summer, he has caught the deliberate rhythms of the stars.

Even more persuasive is the deep spring of water that lies, a great lustrous jewel, in the middle of my largest field. When I am weariest, I go there to drink, and as I lean over the pool — catching the reflection of a tired, hot, anxious face surrounded by summer blue where the clouds are sailing — the water says something to me that is half a rebuke and half reassurance. I ask myself where it comes from — so beautiful

The Cabin Down the Glen

and inexhaustible, never in the least diminished by use or by the longest drought. I ask why it should have come just here, where I need it most, with neither pipe nor pump. It is given, like the air I breathe. All I have to do is to lean and drink.

The farmer who works with me has to tell me many times, in those first days, not to lift my scythe so high, not to bear down on the saw, and not to push on the axe. I think he means that there is something in the nature of a good tool that tries to help one, and that the right use of it is really a kind of leaning or falling, a natural return toward the center. He seems to hint that the whole mass of the planet is waiting to work with me if only I will learn not to get in the way. My task, he suggests, is not a fight but a fellowship. In short, he has faith like that of the pine tree. He draws on a strength not his own, as does the spring in the meadow.

I learn a good deal from this farmer, and not about manual operations only. One day last summer, for example, I had spent an entire morning in a vain attempt to perfect a single paragraph. But my thoughts were in a tangle. My sentences had no music and my rhythms would not harmonize, so that, for one who thinks that prose can hardly say more than it sings, they would not do at all. I was working with only the surface of the mind, trying too hard, striving — as Quintilian once put it — to write better than I could, and I got a full waste-basket for my pains. At last I did one sensible thing: I threw down the pen and strode up the hill and watched this farmer mow a piece of summer grass. Why I should have thought that he could help me, I do not know; but he did.

When I came in sight of him, he was whetting his scythe, making the little valley ring. Then, having brought the blade to an edge that satisfied his thumb, he looked about him for a moment, slowly pocketed the stone, let the two handles of the scythe fall into his palms, and began to swing from his waist, with his arms swaying easily, almost sleepily, from side to side. The snath moved back and forth like a crooked pendulum and the daisied grasses fell in even ranks. They seemed to wish to fall. He sang them to sleep.

The Spring in the Meadow

I said to myself as I watched him: "This is the way the wind works and the planets wheel and the rivers flow. This is not work at all but a kind of dance, a sort of rest. This man is mowing so well because he is not striving. He lets the scythe help him, and the twirl of the earth on its pole. He does not hurry. He is not anxious. He is reaching down below the feeble, fretful, conscious mind to the treasure of his proved memories and true skill. He is like a man singing a song he knows by heart. He works like a good poet for whom rhyme and meter are no longer a hindrance but a help. He is not a blundering tyrant to the grass, but a friend as kind as death. He believes in the nature of things, that they are sound and right and kindly, that they will never leave him or forsake him. O, that I could write as this man mows!"

Then I went back to my cabin, tore up the last of twenty earlier versions, wrote a fresh paragraph as rapidly as the pen would run, and let it stand.

Every day, as I live with the pine and the spring and the farmer, I return a little toward their faith. (For I think it is a return and that all such deeper learning consists in being reminded.) I remember once more what the city made me forget, that every successful effort must be full of rest, as though welling up out of the darkness of sleep, cool, unhurried, and irresistible. My work, when it is good, is like the water that gushes in that spring in the meadow, coming not by its own force at all but on the pulse of subterranean lakes and rivers, on the throb of a vast unimaginable heartbeat. It comes easily and yet because it must, that lifeblood of the planet. Not by any scooping shall I ever get one more drop of water than the spring produces, and not with all my effort can I ever cheat or defeat it. And so with the prose and verse that I write here — is it my task to invent, or laboriously to fabricate wisdom and a beauty never known before? Shall I strive to be "original" in the stupid and shallow sense of that word which is now current?

The Cabin Down the Glen

Why, no; let me rather find out, if I can, what Hesiod and Cato knew. Let me phrase the wordless wisdom of the farmer and the pine tree, and this will seem new to a forgetful and rootless generation merely because it is in fact incalculably old. All the past is strong behind me and all the present is welling round about. It is my business to be a good spring.

Little by little I return to the strong free rhythms. I fall into step with my partners and companions — the wind and rain, dawn and sunset, seed time and harvest — slowly gathering strength for their great stride. Where else should strength come from? Have they not taught us nearly all we know? Did not they make us nearly all we are? When and where did we get this absurd notion that we can prevail without them, even against them, and that we can go alone?

I feel down to the solid earth and trust it to bear me up. I watch the flow of water, seeing that all its beauty and speed is owing solely to the perfect surrender with which it everywhere glides and slips and falls and lets itself go. What does it want most of all, this water of brooks and rivers, this most perfect image of our human happiness and destiny? Why to be drawn down, by the shortest course, from its cradle in the hills to its grave in the sea. I watch the mysterious migrations of birds and recall the belief of W.H. Hudson, who pondered over it for a lifetime, that it too is a kind of falling, and that it answers to the pull of the magnetic poles. I consider the lilies of the field, "how they toil not, neither do they spin." I remember Negro stevedores working on river boats, tramping and swinging to a rhythm, to a song, taking every advantage of the natural tendency of all things to sag, to fall, to sleep. I think of the man I once saw digging trenches through the bone-dry dust of his orange orchard in Southern California, depending upon the water which the mountain had stored for him a hundred miles away. I think of prehistoric men digging dewponds on the tops of the English downs, confident that when once the hollows were made, the water to fill them would somehow come — and come it did, in a way even yet unknown.

But is there any common element in these recollections,

The Spring in the Meadow

analogies, and metaphors? Do they converge to a focus? To me they suggest a most thrilling chance or possibility about this difficult world — one which, if true, would make it far more kindly and homelike. I call it a possibility because my own faith is weak and intermittent, but I have known men and women who never questioned it. Women draw their strength from it when, in the agonies of childbirth, they look squarely into the eyes of Death. To my farmer it is something assured, tried in a thousand ways and never found wanting. Simple persons who live and work with the earth somehow gain and retain this faith; but the loss of it is part of the price we pay for our megalopolitan sophistication and shrewdness. One might almost hazard the guess that it is conveyed by a vague vibration striking upward from the bare soil, which is somehow cut off by city pavements, macadam, and rubber tires. These are non-conductors. If our religion and civilization are now dying, as some think, it may be for the reason that they have been insulated, shut away from the sources of life. It may be that our petty bourgeois, in its contempt for the peasant and the craftsman and its fear of the aristocrat, has been too successful in its effort to turn us all into shopkeepers.

The faith I speak of, which has sustained mankind for ages and is even now the support of many simpler minds among us, is not theological. There is only one article in its creed: It holds that there is an inexhaustible spring in the meadow of the world upon which we may draw for all that we need. There is some Power, it knows, that stands waiting to help, to cheer, and to guide us. I do not care to name it now, for all names are limitations, but I believe that each of the great worships of the world has been addressed to this Power, has been the rediscovery by some direct and penetrative mind of a truth that all right-living men have always dimly known. When we work against this Power, we sin and fail. When we try to work without it, we merely exhaust ourselves. When we work with it, we succeed and fulfill our destiny. I meet it on the physical level when I am learning again to swing an axe. On the mental plane I encounter it in struggling with a refractory paragraph. It is perfectly expressed

The Cabin Down the Glen

in the spiritual range by Dante's line: *e la sua voluntade e nostra pace* [and His will is our peace]. Here is the tap-root of the tree of religion; from this all the pantheons have sprung; and whatever sap there may be in the little theosophies and sham faiths that flutter and fade today is drawn from this. A man who has this faith has religion, no matter what may be his creed or his lack of one; and a man who has it not is an infidel — that is to say, a hopeless, goalless, dying soul — no matter how anxious he may be to do the right things, to find the right creed, to patter the right shibboleth. Well, the sickness of our time, which may well be mortal, is just this: We have lost the faith.

In speaking of levels, planes, and ranges, I do not mean to imply that there is any gradation of dignity between body, mind, and soul. The faith I speak of knows nothing of that hideous dismemberment, that really damnable Arianism, which has torn the human trinity into three. It knows that this inexhaustible Power sweeps through the whole man, so that he may worship as well wielding an axe or while writing a poem as he does when on his knees. There is an infidelity of the muscles, such as I show in my first spring labors, as truly as there is an infidelity of the mind; and this is a perdition of the intellect, such as I exhibit in my effort to write off the surface of the mind, as truly as there is a perdition of the spirit. Yes, and there is a holiness of the body, not at all ascetic, and a sanctity of the mind, by no means confined to the canonized saints, which seems to me identical in nature with that dedication of the spirit which has been singled out for exclusive praise. When water streams down from the snow-covered mountain into the bone-dry dust of the orange orchard, it revives and nourishes the roots, the leaves, and the blossoms, all at once.

ॐ

What shuts us away, then, from these waters and leaves us withering in a prolonged and worldwide drought? Chiefly, I think, it is pride — by which I mean the determination to dominate, to stand alone, to have our way.

The Spring in the Meadow

The assertion that pride can do us any harm will scarcely be accepted in a time like ours. We have forgotten that it was once thought a deadly sin. (Indeed, for that matter, we have forgotten all the Seven Deadly Sins, although we still make shift to practice most of them without knowing their names). We have changed it into a virtue. We call it ambition, self-respect, energy. Indeed, we cannot any longer read *Paradise Lost* intelligently because we no longer admit that the pride of Satan was sinful and a sufficient cause of his expulsion from heaven. Many of us, indeed, consider him the bravely and righteously rebellious hero of that poem — as Milton himself, a city-minded man rather pedantic and very political, by no means remarkable for humility, gave us some reason for our doing. Well, but all the while pride does precisely the same things to us that it did when still recognized as a deadly sin. Namely, it destroys reverence. It shuts us away from Power, as it did Satan. It imprisons us within ourselves, and these selves soon become the equivalent of his hell.

The transformation of our attitude toward pride has not been independent of the Puritan Movement, which John Milton represented in some phases of his complex mind and which the Middle Classes of the western world have never outgrown. Puritanism insulates the individual and at the same time exacerbates his "will to power," so that he is left with nothing but his own crude force to help him and the ignorant supposition that good work can be done in jerks. On the whole a bourgeois thing, city-bred, Puritanism is self-conscious and recent and striving, opposed to the old, the intuitive, and the spontaneous. I sometimes think of it as the Town trying to run the Country. It can only ruin the country — but in this it has already had a terrible success. It has all but destroyed the faith that men once lived by. It hates art and fears dancing. It has no shadow of a realization that all happy and successful living is an art, a kind of dance in which the individual subordinates himself with joy to the mighty rhythms which he does not originate.

Our pride is most obvious on the physical level, where we deal with the mystery called Nature. It shows itself in the

The Cabin Down the Glen

conviction which has grown up in the western world since the Renaissance, that Nature is our slave, to be ruled and exploited for our sole interest. In a recent symposium called Religion Today I read these words of a Professor at Columbia University: "Science has now given man a marvelous control over his physical environment... He has mastered Nature." I do not quote the words because they are brilliantly original but for the opposite reason, because claptrap of this sort is now heard on every hand. A child should be able to see that it is false, and that all we have done toward the betterment of our relations with Nature has been in the way of docile imitation, humble learning, and cooperation. As Aristotle saw long ago, this imitation is the secret of the crafts and of the arts. It is time for us to learn it as the secret of all right living.

The attitude of true science is humble; but true science is an exceedingly rare thing, seldom found among the pick-and-shovel men, whom we dub "scientists," and almost never understood by the laity. For this reason the conviction has gone abroad that we are the tyrants of creation and can do with it what we will. A carpenter, a blacksmith, or a farmer knows better, of course; but what do their opinions matter? We prefer to listen to the little white-collared prophets. We are beginning to imagine that we invented this universe. The old gods are fading from their thrones because we feel no further need of them. There seems nothing left for them to do, now that we have the turbine engine and the concrete mixer. And besides, now that we have the airplane, we need the space.

Before we could figure in our own ignorant eyes as the "Masters" of Nature, we had to lose first of all that old feeling of reverence for her which is evident in all authentic religion and wisdom. This loss, one of the most terrible that the human spirit has had to endure, is to be attributed in part to the struggle of organized Christianity against Paganism. Finding the heathen gods embedded in Nature, it felt obliged to empty that matrix of all holiness and awe. It pointed away from earth toward the sky, never guessing that the one cannot exist without the other. Then came science, tabulating, classifying, measuring,

The Spring in the Meadow

naming things, and always more and more forgetting that its theorems and formulae are mere projections of the mind, ever more assured that in its so-called "laws" it is gradually enclosing and explaining away the whole of Nature's mystery. It came to entertain, or at any rate to convey, a vague notion that it had itself enacted and promulgated these laws. And thus, although it has enormously amplified our conception of the material universe, science has by no means heightened our reverence in the face of that universe or deepened our humility. Rather, it has made us very conceited. Giving us information instead of knowledge, providing us with "higher learning" instead of deeper wisdom, it has led us to think that the two are the same thing. But in reality no amount of information, no conceivable accumulation of facts, can ever amount to knowledge, and doubly true this is when the accumulation is made in an effort toward domination or control. For all true knowledge is cooperative, sympathetic, and essentially humble. True knowledge is a kind of love. It is something that flows into us because we have made a place for it and have taken down all the dams. It is the very antithesis of pride. The farmer with whom I work has a deeper intuitive knowledge of Nature than any professional scientist I have ever known.

After science came its bastard child, invention, and our conceit was heightened by the opportunity this gave us to press buttons and step on levers and so to get results which fools might think their own. Modern industry followed fast, with capitalism to keep it going and to filch the larger share of its reward. Capitalism sees no reason, now that Nature has ceased to be a fane, why it should not be converted into a factory and a slaughter-house. Having ejected the gods, why not turn the hogs loose in the temple? Is it not ours? We killed off the Indians and most of the trees and wild animals. We subdued it. We mastered it. What is to prevent us, then, from smearing the marks of our vulgarity upon whatever natural loveliness may have been temporarily overlooked? The Nature that was once holy has become "natural resources." Where the Greeks in their simplicity, or the Japanese in their heathendom, would have erected an

67

The Cabin Down the Glen

altar to express their reverence for the majesty of Niagara, we set up a power plant — a somewhat different thing.

At present I am concerned with the different effect that the power plant, as compared with the altar, has upon us. It suggests not awe but ownership, and the mood of the slave driver. Now slave driving is even worse for the slaver than for the slave. It brutalizes him. And this is what is happening today. Or rather, this is what has happened.

Whether we can make and maintain a civilization out of a people torn loose from the earth, robbed of her strength and wisdom and the reverence she teaches, we do not know. Whether we can maintain religion without the sense of something greater than ourselves is highly doubtful. The greatest civilizations the world has yet seen are those of Greece, Egypt, and China, and there is this to be observed in them all, that they kept close to the heart of Nature. That custom of the T'ang dynasty which took the Emperor into the fields to drive the plow with his own hands on every vernal equinox, all his court following behind, suggests a reason why China has endured for four thousand years. It was based upon humility. It put first things first. Like Chinese art, it expressed "the fusion of the rhythm of the human spirit with the movement of living things."

Or perhaps I can make my thought clearer by reference to contemporary Russia. There is a nation profoundly reverential and closely bound to the land, full of Nature's wisdom, which a few individuals, city-bred and city-minded, are striving to make over all at once into their own kind. They strike first of all at reverence, as exemplified in religion and in love. They substitute machinery for the old handicrafts and labor with tools on the land. In their schools they do all they can to kill the sense of awe and to enhance man's pride in dominion. Well, they may succeed — precisely as a murderer does — but they will not succeed for very long. Something almighty is against them. In human nature itself there is something that will not

The Spring in the Meadow

indefinitely endure this mechanization, manipulation, and control, not of the outer world only but of itself. There is something deep down in every full-grown human spirit that invincibly demands to be let alone.

The most refractory aspect of Nature, indeed, is that which we find in our own wills. Here too, if we are to work with lasting success, we must be humble, content to work with the grain. Here too we must take Nature as a partner. If we treat her as an enemy, she will surely defeat us soon or late. She hates prohibition and she will not endure censorship. She demands that we work with a positive and persuasive co-operation. Thus, I find that a good way to get rid of weeds is to plant clover. The only permanent cure for ugliness is beauty. The strongest foe of noise is music. Light is the only antagonist of darkness. "If a dog runs at you," said Thoreau, "whistle to him!" There spoke a man who kept the faith.

How might this work out in the field of moral reform, to which the Christian Church is now giving by far too large a part of its energy? Jesus was not much interested in reform, as we understand it. He said: "Seek ye first the kingdom of God," and "Ye must be born again." By the Kingdom I think he meant something like what I mean by the Spring in the Meadow, and being born again was like stooping to drink. Or so I read his words, and this meaning is what I should expect from a simple and penetrative mind, trained in a craft and supported from childhood by the ministries of Nature. He thought that there is something waiting to help us. His teaching is dead against our determination to dominate; it is entirely on the side of reverence, humility, and love. Jesus was no Puritan. If he were here to counsel us about our reforms and our missionary endeavor, certainly he would urge that we abandon our pride first of all, our conviction that we are the people, and that wisdom will die with us. In other words, he would suggest that we turn Christian.

Let us take for example the most obvious effort at reform that has recently been before us — that which Mr. Hoover once very cautiously characterized as "an experiment noble

The Cabin Down the Glen

in motive." The Prohibition Movement may have been noble in motive, but it was hopelessly ignorant in method because it worked against the grain of human nature. It was an effort to dominate. When this dog of intemperance ran at us we began by throwing stones. Ten million dollars thoughtfully spent upon the education of the American people would have made us a temperate nation. We have spent many times that in the effort to supplant one sort of intemperance by another. We thought we had nothing to help us, and were engaged against a hostile universe. Out of our defeat we should at least learn that Nature is not so easily "mastered" after all.

What I am advocating here is something like what Wordsworth meant by a "wise passiveness," and it is not entirely different from what Tolstoy meant to suggest by his injunction, "Stop thinking," and by his marvelous story of the way Kutuzov defeated Napoleon by simply resting down upon the nature of things. I do not assert it as a complete philosophy, but only as that phase of truth to which we need most of all, just now, to attend. I cannot accept the round unquestioning assertion of Emerson: "Place yourself in the middle of the stream of power and wisdom which animates all whom it floats, and you are without effort impelled to truth, right, and a perfect contentment." These are the words of one who never sufficiently learned from his own experience that the lives of most men involve everlasting discipline. They are not muscular and dynamic enough to satisfy the western mind. Their passiveness is not wise because it is not balanced. And yet even this effortless floating of Emerson's is better than the tough struggling which his great friend Carlyle, that intensest of modern Puritans, continually enjoins. He rather disliked currents, apparently, because they do not climb uphill. But the truth is that we ought neither to float without effort nor to struggle toughly. Our duty and our joy is to swim — down stream.

If our civilization is to endure, we must learn to put humility in the place of our pride and reverence in the place of our determination to rule. It is the same thing exactly to say that if our religion is to endure we must subordinate our feverish

The Spring in the Meadow

ethical activity to the spirit of worship. We have to learn what was meant by Thomas Aquinas, chief spokesman of the Ages of Faith, when he said that the contemplation of God is man's highest good and that artistic creation is next to it in felicity. As between the contemplative and the active lives, the relative merits of which were so endlessly debated in the Middle Ages, we must now lay more emphasis than has ever been laid since the Protestant Reformation upon the former. The active and aggressive West must learn once more from the passive and contemplative East, from whence all the major religions have come. It must learn that humble and reverential dependence upon the nature of things, the Tao, which was taught by Lao-Tsze six hundred years before Christ. In all three aspects of our living we must regain our faith that the nature of things is sound and that it will befriend us. We must learn to rest down upon the everlasting arms.

THE DRAUGHT

Cool, deep,
Still as sleep,
Welling from where dark rivers creep,
O crystal water, blood of earth,
In you I drink a second birth.

Strong, slow,
Child of snow,
Through all this creature flash and flow,
That storm and mist and April rains
May mix and mingle in my veins.

Cloud, dew,
Rainbows, hue
Of the under-caverns meet in you.
Fountain of darkness, fallen light,
O beauty woven of day and night,
Carry me back, the way you came,
To caves of calm and skies of flame!

AN OPEN LETTER

Vaucluse, Connecticut
Twentieth Century

To Henry David Thoreau
The Hermitage
Elysian Fields

Dear Sir:

If this letter should revive faint memories of a planet in which you once took a humorous interest, I hope that it will not seriously interrupt your present meditations. For I know very well how it feels, when once a man has found a tiny oasis of quiet in the desert of noise and has set himself down there for a little thinking, to have some raucous voice of the outer world come and quack beside him, impertinently demanding an attention it does not deserve. But wait a moment. I am not writing to ask how you manage to escape boredom with all your time lying idle on your hands, or to inquire whether you are not sometimes lonesome or afraid on stormy nights, or to suggest that you ought to be doing something useful. This letter comes from a cabin standing deeper in the woods than yours did at Walden Pond. It is addressed by one hermit to another; and good hermits, you know, enjoy real society, when they can get it, more than other men. Perhaps you will recall the visit, described by Athanasius, that was paid by that excellent hermit St. Anthony to Paul the Theban, who had lived in the desert even longer than he, and how the two old solitaries were fed by a raven and served by the local lions. Pray consider this letter such another visit as that.

There is, of course, no paradox in the assertion that good

73

The Cabin Down the Glen

hermits are always lovers of their kind. They use all the real society they can get, differing from other men chiefly in the respect that they will not "descend to meet." They insist upon ascending always and upon associating with others, if at all, only on the higher human levels. If the company is somewhat rarefied on the heights, that is not their fault, nor is it even their misfortune. They have a faith that it will always be sufficient.

Your letters, your many noble words about friendship, and even your eloquent silences, show that you knew this. You stood away from humanity only as we do from a mountain, to see its altitude. Sociable, in the cheap and shallow American sense, of course you were not, and Emerson knew whereof he spoke when he said that you were "with difficulty sweet." That hysterical and almost agonized simulation of good fellowship which contorts the faces and skins and the teeth of professional hand-shakers and back-slappers was never seen in you. I have not forgotten the visit of the two itinerant evangelists to your father's house, or how they pawed you over and called you "Henry" during the first evening and inquired about the state of your soul; nor do I forget that after they had gone and you had taken a bath, you simply said, "What good taste the flowers have! They are so reticent!"

And yet you made an unconvincing display of misanthropy. To those you loved you were loving-kind, devoted utterly, and faithful unto death. I wish you had made the fact as clear in words as you did in deeds, so that your friends would not now have to defend you against all that nonsense about falling in love with a shrub oak and about never having found a companion so companionable as solitude. This, of course, was merely "tall talk" and phraseology, hiding the man you were. It reminds me that you lived near the end of the Rhetorical Ages, when a vivid phrase often seemed more important than a sober truth.

But there is nothing peculiar to you in this rhetorical proclivity. I feel it too. We hermits get to imagine that we have to shout in order to make anyone overhear, and this, I suppose, is one reason for our besetting sin of hyperbole. Another fault

An Open Letter

of ours, just as easily understood, is that our writing has too much soliloquy in it and too little conversation so that a hermit's book often gives the effect of one interminable monologue. If we have humor, as you had, then it is likely to be cross-grained. We scold too much, for men who have made the attaining of serenity a main object of their lives, and we fret ourselves by far too much because of evil doers. Again, although we may be in fact as modest as the run of men, we sometimes give careless readers the effect of a smug self-satisfaction or even of arrogance, not only because solitude is in itself a gesture of rejection but because our writings are almost necessarily tuned to the key of self congratulation that we, like Mary, have chosen "the better part." Was it Plato who somewhere said — I think with reference to the Cynics — that "pride is the companion of solitude"? Unquestionably it often is. One of the Christian saints remarked that the hermit in his cell may be as corrupt with pride and vainglory as a dragon in its cave is swollen with venom. It behooves us to consider this. What we want, let us never forget, is not that all men should go into the wilderness and live alone there on locusts and wild honey — for in that case there might not be enough wilderness, not to mention the locusts, to go round — but rather that each man should follow the leading, as we have, of his own highest desire. We would vindicate the liberty of every man to be himself and to conduct his life in his own fashion by defending our own liberty to do the same. But this we do not always make so clear as we should. Temperate and even abstemious in other respects, we sometimes make ourselves amends by a fury of vituperation which our better judgments would deplore. All this, however we shall correct when we come to do our writing over again — for of course an author's heaven is to have all his books brought back to him in the still malleable form of galley proof.

Supposing that you may be engaged even now upon the blissful task of revision, there are certain matters which I should like, with profoundest respect, to point out to you. In the first place, there does not seem to be in your style quite enough of what I call tongue-and-groove work — using an

The Cabin Down the Glen

expression which you, as a carpenter, will at once understand. Finer sentences, to be sure, than your books contain have never been written in America. When you are working happily, your words seem washed in brookwater, the sun pours through your phrases, and your rhythms crackle and snap like a lusty fire of drift-wood. Moreover, your writing is always admirable — honest, muscular, of-the-earth-earthy, as we should expect of one who has just come in from chopping in the wood lot and is all aglow, so that the whole man speaks. You never wrote like one of these professional word-mongers — delicate-fingered, slender-wristed people, all brain and no brawn. You wrote like a good axe-man. And yet the construction of a paragraph or an essay or a book is something different — is it not? — from the chopping of sticks for a stove, so many billets to make a cord. It is more like building, and perhaps it is still more like weaving. Sentences such as yours, so strong and deeply dyed, are excellent material for the loom. Now, what are you going to do with them? For, seriously speaking, you have not consistently woven them together. I know that there are exceptions, but too often you have merely thrown them into heaps, more or less assorted and rather whimsically labeled. Now begins what Rossetti called the "fundamental brain-work." Now comes the toil. Now you are ready to write. And I think that a man who could build a boat or a fence or a table or chair as well as you could will be able to build an essay too, when once he sets his mind to it, in which the sentences and the paragraphs will tongue and groove as though growing out of each other.

Why so exact a man as you were, and withal so self-exacting, did not do this kind of pen-work to begin with, is a little hard to see. Why your carpentry should have been so sound and your paragraphing often so flimsy is a problem. Perhaps we should inquire of Alcott, who gathered wool which he never even spun, and also of Emerson, who taught you the questionable habit of mining your books and essays, bit by bit, out of your private journals. I think you were by gifts and training an accurate close-thinking man, but that, in one sense — and only one — your thoughts kept loose company.

An Open Letter

That walking stick which you cut eighty years ago from a cherry tree sums you up. As a stick it suggests the wanderer that was in you, the man whose fancies went and came like the breeze, in any order and in cheerful defiance of logic; but the two-foot rule that you flattened and notched with inches at the end of it suggests the surveyor, the man who liked to get things right, the man who caught his death of cold while counting the growth rings on felled timber. Well, now, of course a man's style of writing should represent the whole man and not merely that fraction of him — as I feel sure that you will agree — which happens to be in fashion. It should be like a good old coat that has taken the shape of one's person after many seasons of hard and honorable wear and is liberally adorned with patches — preferably not purple. It should be bleached and stained and soaked and dried again in all weathers of a man's mind. And then if people do not like it, they can look elsewhere.

I hope I have made it clear that I, at any rate, like your style, in spite of the fact that you did not always finish your job and sometimes allowed yourself to talk a little wildly. I like the way you have of salting down hard facts, as though you were saying to yourself, "Whatever else may be in conjecture, these things are so." If it is an Irish immigrant in his shanty or the town drunkard or a lonely fisherman by the stream that your eye has chanced upon, you drag that man before us in his habit as he lived. When you look at a woodchuck or at a fox running in snow or at a nighthawk on her nest, you look with such voracious eyes that you give us something more vivid than the thing itself. These pictures burn into the brain. I hardly know where to look in the literature of the world for anything more startlingly actual. And yet, at the very opposite extreme of the mind's gamut, your thoughts were always busy with the mystery of things, asking not what they are but what they mean. You were no mere imagist, a bare sensorium, with no brain above the eyes. You could observe, but also you could think and feel. You did not play on a penny whistle. Overtones of universal significance resound above every note you strike. A fact, dropped into the still water of your mind, woke ripples

The Cabin Down the Glen

there that washed and echoed out to the shores of infinity. Call it style or call it thinking, call it — perhaps best of all — a way of living, I like this sort of thing. I admire it and aspire to it. To the man who can do it, I can easily forgive a thousand peccadilloes and masterly carelessness in matters of verbal structure. Such a man I will read with joy even if I have to do nine-tenths of the work.

Also, I like to read a book that was obviously written by a man, for me. Nowadays we have to write mostly for women, and it makes us "roar as gently as any sucking dove," lest the ladies — God save us! — be affrighted. Or, if we escape this effect of the feminine audience, then we are landed in the cult of deliberate brutality, than which there is nothing more hopelessly effeminate. Henry Thoreau, I hope that you are duly thankful that you lived in a time when whatever culture there was in America had still a noticeable tincture of the masculine.

Your words are like a trumpet heard far-off, appraising us of one man left awake. They have the wild and shagged beauty of the America of our dreams — of that America which is dead now, or sleeping. When I think of the rugged independence, the personal liberty, and the contempt of mere appearances that were once our pride and boast, it is you that I remember — you that have been seventy years in the grave.

Reading your books in the twentieth century is an exciting though a sad experience, because they have been so corroborated by time. Your prophecy of a mechanized American manhood, drab and conventional and afraid, has turned out terribly true. You said that the "mass of men lead lives of quiet desperation," and the only correction I have to make is that their despair is no longer quiet. Since your time they have invented such a huge number of machines, most of them noisy, on which they clatter about over the land or through the air, trying to travel every year a little faster in the vain hope of finally getting away from themselves. By means of other machines they strive to produce every year more "wealth," with the result that just at present one person out of every twelve in America is living on charity.

An Open Letter

Since your time we have had a devastating epidemic of business. You saw the beginning of it and diagnosed the disease, but you could not have foreseen the day in which every stray individual who is not himself infected is looked upon as eccentric. Of late, to be sure, our business men have been given a stiff dose of poverty, and it seems to have sobered those few of them for whom there was any hope; but one observes that their program of "recovery" contemplates nothing but more business, so that we shall probably be obliged before long to get rid of them altogether and try some different fashion in men. "It is well," as you said on your death-bed, "that some things should come to an end."

You foresaw this present, but seeing it is a different thing. You knew the machine only in its infancy and never guessed what a shapeless pulp it would make of human lives. You saw that America had wealth enough and could not foresee that she would have so much that most Americans would be poor. The filth of riches, the poison of power, the madness of crime, and the hopelessness of routine that are now upon us make the times you lived in seem innocent and dewy as the dawn. Our world is immensely older than yours, and wearier. Your faith is to us like a vaguely remembered dream. Strange as it may sound to you, we find you too optimistic. In spite of your violent words, you are too mild for those who face the cruelty of life in our time. —And yet you will be pleased to hear, on the other hand, that certain of our State Universities are excluding your books from their courses in American literature on the ground that you were "radical" and anarchistic. And of course you were. These universities exclude Jesus also, although they do not know enough about him to make the exclusion on similar grounds.

But if the men are worse, the trees are better. In New England, not counting Maine, I suppose there must be ten times as many trees as there were in your day. And although we have not learned to play our part in companionship with the forest, we are beginning. We have a President — think of it! — who has made the intelligent care of trees an important

The Cabin Down the Glen

item of his national policy, as though they were Americans too, and has sent an army of young men into the woods not to slaughter but to save. A hundred years ago there was just one young man in the American woods with any such idea. Now there are a third of a million. The effect of these men on the trees is much, but the effect of the trees on the men is much more. While trees endure there is still hope for men. When I think of such things I am tempted, in my weaker moments, almost to believe in "progress."

On the whole — in spite of the devastations of the engineer, driving his black hard ugly roads through the countryside; in spite of the river killers, stagnating the veins of the earth in huge coagulations upon which they settle like swarms of obscene flies; in spite of the billboard perpetrator and the ubiquitous millionaire — on the whole, I say, New England is a wilder land than the one you knew. You were proud to know the man who owned the horns of the last deer killed in the vicinity of Concord. Well, a full-tined buck stood at the dawn this morning on the hilltop within thirty feet of my cabin. From that same hill I can hear every evening the flight song of the woodcock — one of the wildest and most beautiful things we have, and one which I think you did not know.

Not that it matters much whether you knew this or that fact of Nature, for you were not a naturalist any more than you were what John Burroughs called you, a "wild man." You did not go into the woods and live alone in order to study Nature at closer range any more than you did it in order to escape mankind or to attract attention. The love of Nature was not your main motive, although you had it as a passion in the blood, a sort of holy lust. You went to Walden, as you said, "to transact some private business." And that was? Well, to simplify, to concentrate, to think things out, to uncover essences beneath appearances, to work down to bed rock. Ultimately, your purpose was to go on the quest of your hound and horse and turtle dove, lost forever in the ways of this world but never wholly abandoned. There were times when the woods and fields were to you the diaphanous garment of a Being,

An Open Letter

a Presence, a Power, to which neither you nor I can give a name because the old name has been soiled by much ignoble use, but which we worship, in our way, devoutly. These visions do not come in woods and solitude alone, but they seem to come more frequently there. While we are looking at a tree, a bird, a flower, or a cloud, scales drop from our eyes, and we guess for a flashing unforgettable instant, what lies beyond these things. That is about all that can be said, and if there were more we should not say it. But there is no harm in saying that this sudden vision is what we go into the wilderness to see, and not "a reed shaken by the wind."

What is it that makes a ploughed field in November often more moving to the imagination than a garden in the prime of June? Why is it that the touch of a fern frond in the darkness is sometimes more thrilling than the sight of Niagara? And how are we to account for the sudden exhilaration that often comes from merely grasping a pebble or a clod of earth? The poets and painters and all such dealers in the picturesque have helped us very little toward the explanation of these things. There are moods in which rough young acorns sprouting on an oak are more eloquent with hidden meanings that the rose in all her pride. They speak to a deeper need, to something lying farther down in our memories. Why is this?

You and I believe that there is something beyond beauty, far deeper and stronger and more enduring than the dying forms it wears. And this is what we seek. This, let me hope, is what you have found. Toward this your horse and hound and turtle dove were hastening when they disappeared.

But while we are waiting for it — do you not remember? — there is an everlasting charm and delight in the lesser companionship that the woods can offer. As I write these words I hear the steady drum of rain on my roof. A tiny hemlock, six feet from my window, is dripping water drops from every twig tip. Among its diminutive branches a Maryland yellow throat is quietly exploring, shaking down little showers of rain at every motion of its wings and looking in at me with perfect confidence from time to time. People continue to ask me, as they did you,

The Cabin Down the Glen

what I do here, how I fill up my time, and whether I do not get lonely. Ah, well, the poor we have always with us.

There lies before me while I write a photograph of that little upper room in which the Concord Antiquarian Society has gathered your few belongings together — the bed and chair and writing desk that you made and used, your Indian suit of buckskin, your walking stick and chest and flute, and a book or two about American birds. How bare and honest these things are, and how eloquent of man who took home to himself the noble words: "Within be fed, without be rich no more!" There is not a room in America in which I feel more at home than I do in that one — unless, indeed, it be this room where I am writing now, looking out on a glen full of ferns and boulders, and containing a bed, a table, a hundred books, a piano, and two chairs. That extra chair is a symbol — do you guess what I mean? Though no one should come to visit me for a year, still there it always stands, continually reminding me of what you knew, that although Nature may be very dear, she can never take the place of humanity. I often gaze at it for minutes at a time, filling it in fancy with this friend or that, living or dead; and I wish that you could come this afternoon, Henry Thoreau, and sit there while the shadows gather and sing me your favorite song, "Tom Bowling." For there would not be much that we should need to say. We should listen to the raindrops pattering on the witch hazel leaves by the window, and we should hear the far-off crescendo of the partridge or the tiny thunder that the woodpecker makes on a dead bough. Such sounds have become our language.

The first draft of this letter is written, you may be glad to know, with a pencil bearing the stamp of "John Thoreau & Son." I understand quite well that the Son was far the more important member of that firm — he who had just come home from Harvard, full of Greek and Emerson and other such useless mental baggage. I know how he cut the red cedars with his own hands in the Concord hills, how he invented a machine for the finer grinding of the plumbago, how he took prizes here and there for what was thought "a perfect pencil," thus saving

An Open Letter

his father from a third or fourth failure in business, and then, just when everyone was saying that he might make a fortune, went away to Walden Pond to hoe beans and write a Journal and live on forty dollars a year. —It is not a handsome pencil, just as you were not primarily an ornamental man, but it makes good strong black marks that will last as long as the paper on which they are written.

So will the effect of your thought and courage, sifting down through the years impalpably as star dust scattered on the ages, endure with many Americans while their lives last. It is working today in India, from which so many of your deeper thoughts ultimately came, disturbing the peace of an Empire. I know a young poet, living in a one-roomed cottage in the woods not twenty miles from where I write, who has taken your example and your counsel as his only guide. There will be many such. As the cruel monotony and mechanism of modern life becomes every year more oppressive, they will increase in number, and from every generation you will save a few more young men, awakening them from the dull dreaming of the money grubber and the social climber to something like your own shrewd and practical good sense. Nothing is more certain, as nothing is more wonderful, than the power of honest thought such as yours, honestly spoken, to transcend the centuries and meridians.

Shall I tell you how it happens that I sit here alone in the woods this rainy afternoon, watching the yellow throat in the jeweled hemlock and writing to you? As nearly as I can make out in the bewildering crisscross of life, it is because, many years ago, having earned a half-hour's leisure from my tasks at school, I went to the little library at the back of the schoolroom and there took from the shelf a volume called *Excursions*, written by Henry David Thoreau. I think it was only some strangeness in the author's name, or something faintly adventurous in the title, that first attracted me, for I had never heard or seen either before. By good luck, however, I turned first of all to the essay on "Wild Apples," and it seemed to me as I read that I must have written that essay myself in some

The Cabin Down the Glen

happier incarnation. From there I went on and on until — here I am. Our lives have many beginnings as well as many endings, and I do not wish to assert that the beginning of which I speak was the only one I have known; yet I think I should not be guilty of much exaggeration if I had addressed this letter "To the Man Who Brought Me Here." Certainly I state the exact truth in saying now, at the close, that it comes from one who is

Ever faithfully yours,

O. S.

THE GRAVE OF THOREAU

Brown earth, blue sky and solitude —
Three things he loved, three things he wooed
Lifelong; and now no rhyme can tell
How ultimately all is well
With his wild heart that worshiped God's
Epiphany in crumbling sods
And like an oak brought all its worth
Back to the kindly mother earth.

But something starry, something bold,
Eludes the clutch of dark and mould, —
Something that will not wholly die
Out of the old familiar sky.
No spell in all the lore of graves
Can still the splash of Walden waves
Or wash away the azure stain
Of Concord skies from heart and brain.
Clear psalteries and faint citoles
Only recall the orioles
Fluting reveille to the morn
Across the acres of the corn.

He wanders somewhere lonely still
Along a solitary hill
And sits by ever lonelier fires
Remote from heaven's bright rampires.
A hermit in the blue Beyond
Beside some dim celestial pond
With beans to hoe and wood to hew
And halcyon days to loiter through
And angel visitors, no doubt,
Who shut the air and sunlight out.
But he who scoffed at human ways
And, finding us unworthy of praise,
Sang misanthropic paeans to

The muskrat and the feverfew,
Will droop those archangelic wings
With praise of how we manage things,
Prefer his Walden tupelo
To even the Tree of Life, and grow
A little wistful looking down
Across the fields of Concord town.

GOING WITHOUT

Glad poverte is an honest thyng, certeyn...
Poverte is hateful good, and as I gesse
A ful greet bryngere out of bisynesse,
A greet amendere eek of sapience,
To hym that taketh it in pacience.

— Chaucer

A woman has just been here — a woman, I take it, not unlike those that the hermits of the Egyptian desert hated as they did bishops and feared more than devils. I understand how they felt, although I am certain that they never saw quite her equal. For this was a woman of that earth-cumbering kind that we have recently produced in America, after a hundred years of cosseting and feminolatry, as one of our chief national exhibits. No foreign land could make or would endure such women, and in all the past one meets few of them. Modern comfort, wholly bourgeois and largely American, was necessary to produce them in numbers. There had to be much talk about "rights" and little about duties, there had to be a leisure unearned and therefore unvalued, there had to be pain-killers of many sorts, rich foods in gross excess, padded motor cars, innumerable gadgets, contraceptive devices, and a countryful of chuckle-headed male slaves to keep the whole farce running and to pretend that they enjoyed it, before this creature could emerge in all her graceless ineptitude — unable to bear children, to do any useful work, to think, to talk, to walk, or even to keep still. At the moment, almost the only thing I can find to say in her favor is that she adds a new charm to solitude. When I consider how prevalent and how noisy she is in America, going in and out among the finest women on earth,

The Cabin Down the Glen

I wonder that our woods are not full of hermits.

This particular specimen, I need hardly say, came uninvited. She merely blundered in, having heard that something ridiculously eccentric was going on here that might make good chatter at the club. But I think she was disappointed, for the eccentricities of a man who turns out to be merely poor do not provide much conversation. Having surveyed the few and modest chattels of my cabin — wholly ignoring the ferns and hemlocks and boulders round about — she summed up her impressions in one contemptuous phrase: "No conveniences."

And yet she was wrong in that, because really the convenience of living for some months of every year at least forty miles from her and her kind is to me of inestimable value. My thoughts leaped back, as she spoke, to an amusing letter, almost six hundred years old, written by Lombardo Serico to his friend Petrarch — that is, from one hermit to another. Lombardo describes a visit he has just suffered from a facetious citizen of Padua, who comes into the hermitage with the dull persiflage usually heard on such occasions, pokes about among the few bits of furniture, and finally says, gazing compassionately at the poor couch in the corner: "Do you sleep on that thing?"

Lombardo admits that he does, and very comfortably.

"But what do you eat here?"

"Bread."

"Any meat?"

"I am not a wolf."

"Where is your servant?"

"I choose to live without enemies."

"Why don't you get married?"

"I am a free man."

"Who cooks for you?"

"Fire."

"Who sweeps your cottage?"

"The broom."

"Will you give me a drink?"

"There's a spring in the field over yonder."

"But what do you mean by treating me in this way?

Going Without

What kind of life is this?"
"It seems to me a very good kind of life — when it is quiet."

All things considered, I am glad that this woman came, because the brief and humorous indignation she aroused has set me to thinking about one peculiarity of my life here which might otherwise have escaped my attention — the peculiarity that I do not own many things and that I exert myself rather less than most men do to acquire them. Considered by itself alone, this is a matter of slight interest and no importance. Not one hermit in a hundred, taking all the literature of solitude together, has felt called upon to say a word about it. In America, however, the situation is somewhat different, for it would appear that, with us, mere abstention from society is a far less perplexing thing than refusal to join in the almost universal scramble for material goods. No doubt this is what Thoreau had in mind when, in his book about solitude, he wrote his central and most thoughtful essay on the theme of "Economy." Some explanation of my own attitude seems to be called for, and this will involve a certain amount of self-analysis which, although it may have the look of egoism, is in fact only the necessary statement of a "personal equation."

The man who inhabits this cabin in the New England woods and who gets on happily here — "when it is quiet" — with "no conveniences," first saw the light in a farmhouse of four small rooms and a lean-to in the Mississippi Valley. His father and grandfather were born in log cabins, so that his own present return to an architecture of the same good and wholly American type may perhaps be attributed to what the learned call "atavism." Unfortunately, however, the faith and strength of a true peasantry content with its lot have never been his, unless by a very late learning and adoption. Like all Americans and

The Cabin Down the Glen

most Europeans of the present day, he grew up in a time and a land dominated for good and ill by the middle class — that is to say, by the social estate that invented comfort, businessmen, club women, and all their paraphernalia. His sympathies, to be sure, are not with this class at all, but with the peasant and the peasant's partner, the landed aristocrat who earns and holds his power by inner personal worth. Next to these he respects the craftsman, especially if he works with a tool instead of a machine. These classes he likes and admires because they know things at first hand, because they realize what things cost in terms of human labor, and because they often show the wisdom that can only come of such knowledge. In the few unspoiled representatives of these classes that remain to us, chiefly now in foreign countries, he often finds a humility, a strength won by discipline, and a sense of social solidarity which might yet, if there were enough of them, save modern civilization. But with the successful businessman — that perfect flower of the plant which Luther dibbled and Calvin dunged, he has less affinity than with any other human kind that God lets live — unless it be the successful businessman's wife. (The reference is to the type, of course, and not to individuals.)

Thus, naturally, in a world from which peasants and aristocrats and craftsmen are rapidly disappearing, he finds himself a good deal alone, and for this he tries to compensate by seeking associates in the timeless realms of Mind and Spirit. In other words, finding solitude forced upon him, he has decided to embrace it.

The steady effort of this man has long been to cut across social boundaries and so to escape their limitations, just as it has also been to include all times, all lands, all cultures. He would like, if it were possible, to remain unclassed, as an artist and thinker ought to be. Yet he is well aware that no man can really transcend the ethos into which he is born, that the effort to do so subjects him to terrific strains, and that such success as he achieves is paid for inevitably by a compensating weakness. The strain that he himself feels is sometimes shown in a "great loathing," to use the expression

Going Without

of Nietzsche who had a similar history — a loathing of the noise and squalor and stupidity of modern metropolitan life which he cannot always perfectly control. By sudden heats of anger and outbursts of reviling he shows that he has by no means overcome his middle-class environment or attained the intense serenity of his aspiration. Self-obsession, one of the worst vices of middle-class minds when they are thoughtful, he tries to overcome by humility and sympathetic intuition as he faces the world of Nature and of Spirit and reaches toward the great companions of the past. Perhaps on the whole he is about as bourgeois as Francis Petrarch, the son of an exiled notary, whose life reveals everywhere the strains of a mind uprooted. With Petrarch, indeed, he feels a deep but not wholly admiring sympathy. In memory of that first modern man, so flawed with faults and weakness yet so terribly earnest in the pursuit of noble ends, and in recollection of the beautiful retreat in Southern France where that good scholar and poet sat down, six hundred years ago, to make a wilderness into a solitude by mixing it with mind, he has called his place in Connecticut by the fragrant name of "Vaucluse."

Without the Puritan Movement and the Protestant Reformation this man's individualism would not be quite the same; but on that point it is proper to say that although he was born a Protestant, he now finds himself, without being a communicant or in any way pious, rather more in sympathy with the Catholic tradition. He has a deeper sense of the inherent tragedy of human life and of Nature than is commonly found in the more comfortable representatives of the middle-class. He has no hope that society is to be perfected by public education, by charity, or by social service. He thinks too well of God to believe that vox populi, at any rate as it is now heard in America, is a close equivalent of vox Dei. On the whole, he expects catastrophe and would prefer to have it come soon. The patching and tinkering of the old economic machine that is now going forward interests him intensely — and leaves him more than ever convinced that what we really need is a new machine, or else none. Such hope as he has for western

The Cabin Down the Glen

civilization does not rest upon science, invention, business, reform, or democracy, but upon the individual mind and soul. The courage and beauty and strength of a few human spirits he has known have been by far the most amazing discoveries of his experience, but he does not deduce from them any admiration of humanity in the mass. He does not share the ludicrous bourgeois notion that we have "conquered nature," and he has no expectation or desire that we shall ever do so. He does not estimate the value of his life, or of any life, by financial profit and loss, by social reputation, by what is called "service" or by what is called "respectability." This descendent of American pioneers is now trying to concentrate the scattered and restless energy of his forefathers upon the inward frontier — partly in order to round out his own life and partly because he is utterly convinced that America's supreme task of spiritual and intellectual self-exploration and self-conquest is now inescapably upon her. Failing here, she fails everywhere; and she is at this moment the wildest, least disciplined, the most childishly unrestrained and self-ignorant people that has ever in history been called civilized. This man, a wanderer by nature and experience, is now, by force of will, an in-trailer, like Thoreau. He believes that the highest service any man can render to his fellows is that of quiet example. To this end, leisure, which Protestantism destroyed in its higher aspect and is now getting back again in a grievously degraded form, is for him the goal of labor; and the self-cultivation which leisure makes possible, that high ideal of the Renaissance, seems to him a sufficient and utterly unselfish program for a lifetime. He has eased the obtaining of leisure and its opportunities by happily going without most of the things that most men want. He has adopted Poverty, in part as a matter of good taste and partly because it saves time. — Or, on second thought, she may have adopted him. Who knows? And after all, what does it matter, except for the statement of one's personal equation? One does what one can with the crude stuff that life offers.

∂•

Going Without

During most of the centuries that we call "Christian" and "modern," a single unvarying but steadily hardening theory with regard to worldly possessions has been all but universally held. It is true that a certain young enthusiast in Judaea once preached, and even practiced, a quite different theory. He was utterly earnest about it — indeed a little too earnest, and it might have been better for us if he had tempered his austerity with humor and winged his message with a smile. At any rate he left no one, and certainly no one among his own followers, the slightest excuse for ignorance of his opinion. Again and again he returned to the topic, which lay close to the heart of his whole teaching, showing unmistakably by precept and proverb and parabolic example what he considered the spiritual effect of devotion to this world's goods.

And with what result? Most of those who have called themselves the followers of this Teacher decided some time ago that his theories on this topic, as on a good many others, were, to say the least, visionary and impractical, better suited to Sunday profession than to week-day observance. Some have tried to show that he did not really mean what he so clearly said, and others that if he had lived in our time he would have said just the opposite of what he did say; but most of his followers in recent centuries have found that it saves mental effort simply to ignore this part of his teaching altogether. So far from accepting his views about "holy poverty" and the slim eschatological chances of millionaires, they have tended rather, since the time of John Calvin, to consider the possession of great riches one of the least dubitable marks of divine favor. Qualities of mind and character making for success in the pursuit of riches they have come to regard not at all as vices but as virtues. It is curious to observe that many of them who are most severe in their censure of all excesses and irregularities in the amative instinct, about which their Teacher said nothing, are almost worshipful before debauchees and perverts of the acquisitive instinct, which has done vastly more harm in the world than the other and concerning which the Teacher said a great deal in the way of solemn warning. In fact we must

The Cabin Down the Glen

set it down as one of the oddest outcomes of history, that the time and place in which the lust for wealth burns most fiercely is that very Christendom founded by One who had not where to lay his head. The heathen contract this libido from us as a main characteristic of our contemporary Christianity. And so it seems really to be. It is increasingly difficult to discern the dim and ancient emblem of the Cross beneath the vivid Dollar Sign on the banners of our Christian soldiers.

With the various pagan philosophers, voluntary paupers, and other negligible persons who have advanced opinions like those of the Judaean Teacher we need not concern ourselves. As every one knows, the orthodox view has long been that "goods" of all kinds are unquestionably good; that the main thing to do with them, and indeed the main thing to do with life, is to acquire and own them, whether by inheritance or by simple appropriation or, when necessary, by some other more laborious mode of acquisition; and that the more one owns of them, the better off one must be. — But why stop at saying "the better off" when what we really mean is "the better?" So confidently is this orthodox doctrine applied that we often try to estimate the worth of a man by finding out what he is "worth" in stocks and bonds, houses and lands, dollars and cents. Whatever we may profess on Sundays about the superior advantages of poverty, our underlying conviction is tersely expressed by Tennyson's Northern Farmer: "Take my word for it, Sammy; the poor, in the lump, is bad."

Charmingly simple, is it not? — this doctrine that turns a billion wheels, fills the day with clatter and the night with toil, blurs the blue of the sky and smears the landscape with vulgarity, drags the world up betimes in the morning and drops it exhausted into bed. Simple it is, and suited to the childish comprehensions from which it first came, without being in any good sense childlike. One may say that it keeps the world running, though quite possibly in the wrong direction. One may say that it keeps a great many people — not by any means all of those for whom it is responsible, however, — busily employed, though frequently at tasks that might better not be done.

Going Without

What we may not say of this doctrine is that it makes people happy. As Huai-Nan Tsu remarked over two thousand years ago, "Men are now as miserable as though all were over with them. And this is because they use outward things as a means of delighting their hearts, instead of using their hearts as a means of enjoying outward things." And another claim that we may not make for this doctrine is that it provides the only sensible view of worldly possessions. It seems orthodox and unquestionable only because it has not been recently assailed. Satire, if we had any, might tear it to tatters. A manly heart-whole laughter, if that too were not gone, might blow it to bits.

Stout and firm as this orthodoxy looks to us, we may well doubt whether it is deeply rooted in human nature. Not by any means so universal in distribution as we commonly suppose, it seems to have spread from the northern temperate zone; and even there it is hardly normal, but may be regarded as a morbid hypertrophy of the instinct which impels the non-hibernating animals to lay by some store against the winter. A man who lives for the gathering of possessions is therefore somewhat like a squirrel gone mad, dashing about and burying nuts in miscellaneous directions, burying a thousand times as many nuts as he can ever eat, and straightaway forgetting where he puts them. In terms of time this disease is surprisingly recent. Although the Phoenicians seem to have suffered with it considerably — that is almost all we know about them — and Venice in her best days had a virulent attack, it has been really endemic only since the Protestant Reformation. In social range also it is, or once was, narrowly restricted, having begun with the lower middle classes of Europe and having retained its petty bourgeois characteristics ever since. To say that it has steadily spread and is today to all appearances universal is only another way of saying the obvious thing, that we are now ruled, and have long been, by shopkeepers. What is not quite so obvious is that this class, which has monopolized all that it cares for, has never even tried to gain a monopoly upon wisdom. Other views about what we are here for and what makes life worth living have been held in the past by sensible men, and

The Cabin Down the Glen

may be held again. As I read the news from Russia — and also the news from France, from Germany, from England, and even from that America which we have always proudly regarded as the land of the businessman and home of the rich — this bourgeois philosophy is beginning to show signs of wear. Before the present decade is out, a great many millions who have never thought of doubting that the main purpose of life is the collecting of personal possessions may find themselves considering the merits of some totally different idea.

What we regard as the only possible attitude toward wealth is in fact no more than a "doctrine," in the special sense given to that word by the English thinker T.F. Hulme. That is to say, it is one of the theories which we take for granted, allowing them to govern our conduct without ever subjecting them to close examination. All other things of heaven and earth we see through these doctrines, as though they were windows of very imperfect and distorting glass, but the doctrines themselves we never see. Or, in another way of putting the matter, this endless and earnest getting of things upon which we expend nearly all our powers is just a game — often, let us admit, an exciting one, although it must grow a little monotonous after half a century — which we play as if there were no other.

And yet there is, as a matter of fact, another game quite as interesting as this one, — older, less laborious, less exacting of time and energy, more permanently enjoyable, and in every way more in keeping with the canons of good taste. For purposes of contrast with the Game of Getting, at which nearly every one is now eagerly at play, we may call it the Game of Going Without.

This diversion is not restricted to any one social class, period of time, or geographical habitat. The hermits of the Egyptian desert played it with enthusiasm seventeen centuries ago, strictly observing all the rules, and the anchorites of the Middle Ages gave themselves up to it with all the ardor to be found today among the gamblers in Wall Street. So did Thoreau at Walden Pond. So, for at least three thousand years, have many millions of saints and thinkers in the forests of

Going Without

India. Diogenes played this game in his tub at Corinth and Abraham on the plains of Namre. Once when Confucius was climbing Mount T'ai, he saw an aged man roaming about near the summit clothed in deerskin, girded by a rope, and singing gaily to himself as he played his own accompaniment on a lute. Confucius asked him what he was so happy about. "Why," said the ancient, "there are several things. In the first place, God made man the noblest of animals, and it has been my good luck to be a man. Next, some of those who are born never see the sun and moon or even leave their swaddling clothes, but I have walked the earth for ninety years. Further, poverty is the scholar's natural condition, and death is the end appointed for us all. Well, I have always lived in this normal state, and now I am rapidly approaching the goal that all men seek. What more does a man want to make him happy?"

Emphatically, then, the good Game of Going Without is not now for the first time invented. It has only been forgotten. To revive it again we need only a few such exemplary persons as the sage Lao-Tsze, who, after gazing long and quizzically at the Game of Getting as it was played in the Imperial City six centuries before our era, decided that it was not good enough. By this he meant, quite simply, that it did not yield what all men seek — happiness. His decision, so often recalled by Chinese painters and poets, set him and his innumerable disciples at last on the right Way. "One may see the Way," he said, "without looking out of the window. The more one travels the less he may know." And I think he would have agreed that the more one gathers the less one may have.

For the Game of Getting takes up nearly all one's time, and that is what no mere game, however exciting, should ever be allowed to do. By definition, a game is a diversion the purpose of which is to distract attention temporarily from the more serious concerns of life, whatever we take them to be. That man must be an utter fool, or else too pusillanimous

The Cabin Down the Glen

a conformist to call his life his own, who spends all his time on a game — and whether it be the game of golf or that of collecting dollars does not matter. Furthermore, when once a man has collected a considerable surplus of dollars, then there is the additional trouble of keeping them, the fear of losing them, and also — among the newly rich — the half-ludicrous and half-pathetic anxiety to "live up to" them. Surely, if the angels do really weep and the devils laugh, the spectacle of a human being trying to show himself worthy of the heap of metal he has accumulated gives them their opportunity. Worst of all, we can hardly play this game very long without injury to our sense of humor — without slipping into the naive belief that these things are important in themselves, and that we become more important in proportion as we collect them and paste them more or less decoratively about our persons. This is so obvious an absurdity that it becomes a wonder how anyone can play the Game of Getting without laughing at himself and his fellow players most of the time. That, indeed, is the only safe way of playing it; but it is rare.

Going Without, on the other hand, is a game all drenched and charged with humor. One might even say that humor is its very essence, for the players of it see things in their right proportions and are skillful in estimating relative values. They put first things first. Leisure, independence, and happiness are first things, which they have no thought of subordinating to houses and lands and bank accounts. Constantly they ask themselves how much of their leisure and independence such and such a piece of personal property would be worth to them; and often they answer: "Not one minute."

Thus it is clear, or should be, that in spite of their apparent unworldliness they are shrewd bargainers after all. They are determined never to pay a penny too much for any whistle the shops of the world have to offer. To take an example: No businessman in Boston, eighty years ago, was a better economist than Henry Thoreau of Concord, who never had anything to do with business in the usual sense that he could avoid. The skill and the knowledge and the Yankee shrewdness

Going Without

that his contemporaries spent in piling up possessions and in buying their brownstone fronts on Commonwealth Avenue he used in discovering how much of the world's good he could go without and be the richer for so going. He built the house of his content with cheap and few materials, most of which he picked up in the woods, yet it was a good house for his uses. He knew how to make ends meet. Furthermore, he never made the stupid mistake of confusing ends with means. He put first things first, and that is all that the higher economy amounts to: It rests upon a sense of order and of relative values.

Thoreau, of course, considered himself a wealthy man, and so do I. In another place I have spoken with gratitude and, I hope, a becoming humility, about my opulence in such really good things as fire, water, seeds, tools, words, music, and books. It has been precisely by going without a clutter of superfluities, miscalled "conveniences," that I have come to realize how good these are. When I step down to my spring in the meadow and dip out a cupful of that beautiful water, standing for a moment before I drink to watch the play of sunlight in the bottom of the cup, how can I feel poor? While I hear the hermit thrushes hallowing the quiet of a June evening here in this peaceful glen, how can I envy the man who lives in a palace on Fifth Avenue? And when I am sitting by my hearth in the cabin on a winter night, with a book in hand and the fire prospering and my tall iron candlesticks beside the chair, warm and quiet and free, molesting no man and unmolested, with my thoughts ranging up and down all space and time, is it to be supposed that I feel in any way inferior to the wretched creature who, in these last few years of economic disaster, by sharp practice and betrayal of trust and the use of every legal loophole, has added more millions to those which already he did not know what to do with? Why no; it is rather pride from which I must strive to save myself and that insidious hardening of human sympathies that good fortune too often brings.

How delightful it is to go without things can hardly be guessed by those who have always played the Game of Getting. It is like being clean. To travel light, to have so few

The Cabin Down the Glen

"conveniences" that one is never inconvenienced, to enjoy what others merely own — these are advantages that need no argument. And this frugality, moreover, is always in good taste, whereas opulence has an almost fatal trend toward the vulgar. Add the fact that those who play this game have a good deal of time left over for something else, for going without things is not time consuming.

We have heard it said many times, but the truth does not wear out, that the palaces and pictures, the vast estates, the rich houses and lordly furniture and noble books of the world belong to him who can most deeply enjoy them; and that person is likely to be he who has the least wish to possess them in any shallow and fictitious legal sense. Rich men are his factors and agents. He is the final consumer. With regard to the higher class of goods the folly of the acquisitive instinct is even clearer. Who owns the sonatas of Beethoven, and who possesses the sunset and the poetry of Virgil, or who has taken out a title-deed to the song of the hermit thrush? Not I, certainly, although I extend my claim upon them a little every year. The only title I care about even to these acres of Connecticut that are legally called mine is that I love and cherish them, I do verily believe, as much as any man on earth could do.

In all of this, chiefly because it has been so often said and so seldom attended to, there may seem to be a touch of mere rhetoric if not of insincerity. Perhaps I should say once more, then, that I have no intention of going without any good thing that I can get at a reasonable price, and that I have no wish to impoverish my life, but a strong wish to enrich it. There is, indeed, an important sense in which it is every man's duty to be rich — that is, to own all the things he can really enjoy and use and absorb into his mind and character. At present, if I may say so without boasting, I possess all these things. In fact, I have a superfluity.

In his prayer to Pan at the end of Plato's *Phaedrus*, Socrates

Going Without

asks that his store of gold may be such as only a wise man may endure. I have never been quite sure what he meant, because it is clear that a wise man can bear up both under a wealth and also under a poverty that would quite crush and extinguish a fool. From one point of view it might seem that every man should be given as much of the world's wealth as he can administer for the common good, and that those to whom riches would be a source only of madness or of a stupid pride should be deprived of them altogether. But why must we always discriminate against the wise? It is better, probably, to let each man be as poor, in the ordinary meaning of that word, as he is able. Not only does this give nearly all the material wealth of the world to those who have no other way of making sure that they exist, but it involves the least disturbance of the present arrangement. Thus the lovely phrase that the Greeks so often used in their epitaphs for the dead will remain applicable to the living sage: "Lie lightly, gentle earth!"

IN A SILENCE

Ah, listen now!
No zephyr stirs the hemlock's top-most bough;
The ferns are green-gold sculpture down the glen;
There comes no echo from the world of men;
And every vocal bird has flown away
Into some other chamber of the day.

Clear, dark, and deep
These waters are, these wells of ancient sleep
Where slumber all
The voices of all yesterdays — each cry and call,
Each old forgotten glory of clamant strings,
And music's utmost inward murmurings.
This is the pregnant, still, mysterious word
That John on Patmos heard,
And Moses on the peak of Sinai
Enisled amid mute solitudes of sky.
This is the secrecy God hearkened to
While yet his unstarred sky was empty blue;
And this that lonely Listener shall hear
After the ceasing of the last faint sphere.

Of every sound this is the hollow womb.
Of every dying tone this is the tomb.
O Alpha and Omega! This
Is the end in the beginning, the abyss
From whence we come and into which we go.

Confront it, then, lone heart of mine, and know
Its downmost depth and dark. No grave can be
More still than this.
                    Now is Eternity.

The leaves droop breathless on the aspen bough.
Ah, listen! Now!

102

SOLIPSISSIMUS

These are events: the heavy bees that drone
Among the asters at my window-pane,
The chipmunk darting from his door of stone,
The whistle of a far hill-climbing train,
The vireo that shakes a hemlock cone.

And these are thoughts: the blue of the aster-bloom,
The larger blue of a wide cloud-lighted sky,
Broad ferns that feed all day upon the gloom
Of the listening glen, and bracken five feet high,
Breathless as pictures in a painted room.

Now whether bee and bird wings only fly
Across this inner landscape of the brain,
Or whether, strange and distant utterly,
They beat some outer air, I ask in vain —
And whether trees bear leaves, or solely I.

Yet this I know: Whatever worlds may loom
Beyond the still thought where I sit alone
Come creeping back into the mental womb,
As though the vast last trumpet had been blown
And this were immortality, and doom.

WITH HATCHET AND
PRUNING SHEARS

The wind was loud among the tree tops while I worked this morning in my spinney of gray and white birches. It caught the flashing little leaves in bundles and by armfuls, dashing and clashing them together, bending them downward, rending them upward, scattering them excitedly apart; yet to me, deep in the thicket of slim glimmering stems, the wind was hardly more than the voice of ocean heard from the hollow safety of a ship's hull. The June day glittered and glanced just overhead, but I worked in a tremulous green twilight that was raveled and rewoven every moment out of shade and shine. A gay place and time it was, brimming with leaf-music, bristling with life.

Never have I been more aware of the lunge and thrust and jet of life, or of its blind determination to bear down all restraint. That same compelling onward impulse which binds and blends male and female, ages deeper than consciousness, was at work here too, in all its tyranny. Not that one could blame it, here or elsewhere. "Male and female created He them." The rest — follows.

Earth seemed to be boiling with birch trees. Clearly it was the wish and will of that young wood that every square foot of my acres should be covered with nothing but birches; and when that had been accomplished, they confidently intended to go on from there and occupy the remainder of the planet. But I had other notions.

Let it be understood that I am very fond of birch trees, especially when a high wind sets them dancing; yet hemlocks are good trees too, and I like hickories just as well. Birches are a stiff-necked, not to say an insolent, generation. One of

With Hatchet and Pruning Shears

them standing alone is docility itself, and even half a dozen in a clump are often comely and well-behaved, but let a thousand of them once get together and they become a mob, swiftly developing the ugliest traits of all ungoverned multitudes. Here were ten thousand at least. Having entrenched themselves on the hill-slope, they were pouring into the valley and swarming toward the summit, killing almost every other tree that fell in their way. This they did not by individual strength, as a great oak may overpower all other vegetation in its neighborhood, but by sheer ignoble mass and number. They were a democracy slipping toward communism. The species throttled the individual and tree was strangling tree. In short, the situation in that spinney was very like what any unbigoted person with his eyes open may see going on in American or European society today. What the trees needed, as every multitude does, was a ruler, for they had utterly failed to rule themselves according to the absurd principle that one birch is as good as another and that all trees are created free and equal. More fortunate than America or Europe, they had such a ruler at hand.

The thicket, some six hundred feet in length, was so dense that I could make no progress through it except on all fours, and then only with some laceration of hands and face. Seen from the outside, it was a shapeless mass of verdure, a green chaos. Within, the stems stood so close together that in many places a rabbit could hardly have run between them. Their black and leafless lower branches were tangled together. From spring to autumn, no sunshine ever fell on the ground there. The flowering laurel shimmered ghostly white in the shadows, having grown in a day-long dusk.

It is amazing, the improvement that can be made in a few moments of careful trimming upon a birch that has grown among many others. One finds it with the bark disfigured by scores of short black branches, all quite dead, and with many twigs of lighter hue that mar its symmetry. It is a hirsute, nondescript, ill-conditioned vegetable that seems to need most of all a sharp axe laid at its root. But let the pruning shears flash in and out, up and down, for three minutes, and what

The Cabin Down the Glen

seems another tree stands forth — slender, tall, maidenly, white as sea-foam. Its very motion is different now, as it sways more freely in the wind. For the first time it reveals its deeper nature, like a shy girl who knows at last that she is loved.

Working my way along the spinney, letting in the day, opening vistas here and there, I felt something of the artist's delight; for if it could not quite be said that I was creating beauty, at least I was uncovering and interpreting it. Where no one had been able to walk for years, I was driving a path; bits of landscape that no one had ever seen I was opening out; upon the raw material provided by nature I was stamping a human pattern. My purpose was to cut a footpath as nearly as possible through the middle of the thicket, which is much longer than it is wide, and in doing this I found that I could make openings for many glimpses into the country lying uphill and down. There can be few things better to look at than a wide landscape framed between the slender boles of young birches, swaying in the wind with all their banners streaming. Many such I found and framed this morning as I toiled through my tunnel of leaves.

These were not the only surprises that I had. At almost every yard of progress I came upon some infant flower or shrub or tree that was doomed, except for my help, to an early death. Hundreds of seedling pines and tiny beeches were struggling for breath there, besides innumerable bushes of pallid laurel. To each of these I have given its share of light, so that there is now good hope that when the birches have lived out their brief term, a grove of pines will take their place. While I was resting in the shadows, a company of black and white creeping warblers, great lovers of birches, came leaping and fluttering among the boughs just overhead, and a hooded warbler ran about among the ferns within six feet of where I lay. Most surprising of all, I heard a faint lisping sound at the farther end of a branch on which my shears were already resting, and then saw, less than a yard away, a very young catbird — or should one say a "kitten bird"? — staring at me with round unblinking eyes. I spared that branch.

With Hatchet and Pruning Shears

But what was I doing there? Well, not to put too fine a point upon it, I was cutting trees — a capital crime in the eyes of all our "passionate lovers of Nature." At the very least, I was taming the wild, and so was sinning greatly against the code of those who think that Nature can do no wrong and that man never raises his hand against her except to ruin or mar.

Between lovers of the wilderness and lovers of the man-handled rectilinear park and garden, the controversy is ancient, eager, and never-ending. No two countries or centuries or even individuals decide exactly alike upon the question, deeply significant and philosophical, whether it is better to give Nature her free course or to rule and dominate her severely. Classical periods, delighting in all evidences of man's power, like to see her subjugated, trimmed, reduced to precise geometric designs; but Romantic epochs prefer the wild, the spontaneous, the "natural."

In America the controversy is exacerbated by the fact that almost all our dealing with nature thus far on this continent has been destructive. There seem to be three normal stages in any society's relationship with trees: butchery, sentimentality, and control. Considering that by no means all of us have yet passed out of the first of these and that very few have entered the third, it is a probable assumption, when a man is seen cutting trees, that he is bent upon murder. But for my own part, although I can understand it, I cannot help resenting this imputation when it is leveled at me. No sentimental tree worshipper, I believe, has ever mourned the deaths of noble trees more than I have, or has lain awake longer at night when the smoke of forest fires was in the air. No one has ever read Ronsard's plea to the woodcutters for his Forest of Gastine with more sympathy, or Victor de Laprade's three superb elegies on a fallen oak, or Cowper's Poplar Field — preferably in the Latin version. The fact is, I think that I love trees as much as anyone can — and that is the reason why I went forth this morning armed with hatchet and pruning shears. Because a man is a philanthropist, we should not expect him to approve everything, murder included, that human beings do to one another. On the

The Cabin Down the Glen

contrary. And for the dendrophile the same rule holds.

But here again I cross the conviction — an ignorant and feebly sentimental one, as it seems to me — of those who believe that Nature can do no evil, that "all her ways are ways of pleasantness, and all her paths are peace." This notion, with its vague aesthetic and theological corollaries, did not appear in the world during the long ages when we had to keep a steady eye on Nature, knowing full well that she was not to be trusted. It is, in fact, not much more than a century old. Beginning with a group of Romantic poets and philosophers who praised the wilderness chiefly in order to dispraise society, it has been greatly spread and strengthened — but not justified — by such apparently irrelevant inventions of recent decades as central heating, antisepsis, and the use of anesthetics. Until we had shut ourselves away in city streets from savages and wild beasts and the north wind of winter, until most of us had quite forgotten the fear of hunger and nakedness, until we had learned to huddle out of sight and therefore out of mind — but not out of existence — the more painful spectacles of human suffering and insanity and idiocy and crime, it never occurred to us to tell this pleasant lie. Farmers and woodsmen, physicians and surgeons, and those others among us who still face Nature squarely do not tell it now. It is chiefly comfort, that highly questionable modern discovery, that has lulled us into our stupid error. One can understand how a swathed and cushioned bourgeoisie, living the life of lap dogs, as devoid of imagination as it is of first-hand experience, can conclude that, because its belly is full and its skin warm, God must be in his heaven and all must really be well with the world. And one can understand even better how the overfed and under-worked of our "upper middle classes" — those from whom rather too many of our current beliefs and shibboleths are derived — have been led to generalize unwarrantably upon their own soft and coddled existence. Even for them, to be sure, there remain such stark uncompromising natural phenomena as cancer and death in childbirth, but for these they manage to find some anodyne or soporific, some screen to stand between them and reality,

With Hatchet and Pruning Shears

some pseudoreligion, which enables them to go on lying about the facts. Meanwhile the facts remain precisely what they were before — from the human point of view, which is all that matters, rather horrible.

What would these Nature worshippers have thought and felt, I wonder, about the spectacle I came upon in the woods a few days ago — a hawk eating a goldfinch? That sight left a vivid stain in memory, and not for itself alone but because it was emblematic of something inherent in Nature which is revolting to every sensitive mind. As I stood there, forcing myself to gaze at it and to learn its hard lesson, I realized quite clearly, not for the first time, that there is a deep gulf, however it may have been made, between Nature and the higher spirit of man. Let the sentimentalists personify Nature as they will, calling her our "mother" and our "homely nurse," but she is the kind of mother who eats her children in ways too foul and cruel to bear thinking of. Let the materialists and the "behaviorists" go on asserting that we ourselves are on all fours with the beasts of the field and that there is nothing in us which does not come from Nature, but I should like to have them explain what it was in me that shuddered at the sight of that gorging hawk. I choose to think that it was something which Nature knows nothing about, something she did not make and never allows for, something different — something, in short, human. A psychologist would probably tell me that I shuddered at that spectacle because, in some sense and degree, I dramatized it; and this would be true. I raised it to the level of our human tragedy and made it the symbol of all our unearned and profitless suffering, but I do not see that this rendered it any the less perfect an example of Nature's cruelty. I became that goldfinch (And yet why not the hawk as well? Do I want hawks to starve?) exultantly flying and singing one moment in the sunshine, and then suddenly brought down in the claws of some unguessed creature pouncing with a shriek out of the sky that had seemed my sheltering home. Yes, I dramatized the incident. I saw it as typical of what we all have to expect.

Algernon Swinburne once expressed a thought and

The Cabin Down the Glen

feeling similar to mine in a phantasia upon a theme from William Blake. He lashes himself into a finer frenzy and cries out against Nature with more violence of rhetoric than I should care to use, but still it seems right that a poet should be allowed some vociferation in taking back and unsaying the hoary lie about "Mother Nature" that so many poets have ignorantly told. "Nature averse to crime!" he shouts. "I tell you Nature lives and breathes by it; hungers at all her pores for bloodshed, aches in all her nerves for the help of sin, yearns with all her heart for the furtherance of cruelty... What subsides through inert virtue she quickens through active crime; out of death she kindles life; she uses the dust of man to strike her light upon; she feeds with fresh blood the innumerable insatiable mouths sucking at her milkless breast... Friends, if we would be one with Nature, let us continually do evil with our might. But what evil is here for us to do, where the whole body of things is evil? A few murders. A few."

To speak somewhat more quietly, no decent and thoughtful man who knows what he is talking about can wish to be "one with Nature" in the sense of accepting her blind and lustful will as the model of his own. The "return to Nature" of which we have heard by far too much since the time of Rousseau would really mean the rejection of the best that man has gained in his long climb. Such a return would be at least as ruinous as the principle upon which we have thus far worked has proved to be — the principle which finds sanction in those words of Genesis: "And God blessed them, and God said unto them, 'Be fruitful, and multiply, and replenish the earth, and subdue it; and have dominion over the fish of the sea, and over the fowl of the air, and over every living thing that moveth upon the earth.'" To "subdue" and to "have dominion" — there is the other extreme, as false and almost as destructive as the modern Romantic idea of sinking down into the landscape. I see how it applies to the Nature that rebels in our own members, but I also see that in its application to the outer world it has laid earth waste and has made us ignorantly conceited and has left us weak and helpless. Why is it necessary, after all, that

With Hatchet and Pruning Shears

man should be either a slave or a tyrant? Why may he not be Nature's partner, learning all he can from her and teaching her what she has no other way of knowing? That was what I tried to do this morning in my spinney of birch trees.

A main trouble with most praisers of the wilderness is that they have never seen any wilderness whatever. They know nothing, either by personal participation or by imagining, of that ancient war between men and trees which is still going on in many parts of the world — a war in which trees of some kind are quite certain to win in the end. One glimpse of a full-grown jungle would convert them, but they never get that glimpse. They prefer to remain at a safe distance from the wilds they ignorantly praise.

As in nearly all such disputes, the best course lies in a golden mean, and I am as cold to all suggestions for letting these acres grow completely wild — for if I did that I should soon have to move out — as I should be to a proposal to turn them into a formal park. It seems to me obviously stupid and ignorant to assert, with the ultra-Romantics, that men can never improve upon Nature. The meadows he has made are far more beautiful, as well as more serviceable, than the swamps from which they come. A glade of oaks or beeches tended by human care and intelligence is far lovelier than any haphazard woodlot, and more cheerful by far than such bits of primeval forest as we have left. And yet it is equally clear that human control can be carried too far, as it was in the rather absurd topiary landscape gardening of the Italians. The best effects are secured by a collaboration in which the human instinct for order works together with Nature's apparent caprice in securing results that neither of the two could have achieved alone. Such effects are found at their best in the southern counties of Old England, where men have best understood the rewards of this partnership, or have understood them longest. The beauties of these counties are so rich and manifold because of the harmony worked out there between two diverse yet friendly forces, and the eye delights to trace in them the contribution of each.

In New England we have still to acquire both knowledge

The Cabin Down the Glen

and taste before anything like this cooperation can begin on a large scale. It is true that anyone who knows the country thoroughly, in the walker's way, can remember many communities in which trees and men have dwelt together for a long time on terms of mutual forbearance if not of friendship, but in general we are just ceasing to think of trees as the enemy. The history of our dealing with what was once the noblest forest on earth is heartbreaking to consider. It has brutalized us all. The tree butchers are still with us in great numbers and power. (One of them had cut several hundreds of the finest trees on my acres four or five years before I came here, leaving his slashings in huge ugly piles to cripple the young growth and increase the hazard of fire.) Their brutality breeds sentimentalism, which is the same thing turned inside out.

Such is the aspect of the present situation, and when I think of it alone, I almost despair, seeing in terrified fancy an America of three hundred years hence denuded like modern Spain, parched, poverty-stricken, a dreadful skeleton. Even now we have scarcely any margin of safety, yet we go on spending out of mere dissolute habit like a man who has once been a millionaire and so does not take the trouble to find out what is his present balance at the bank, the chief difference being that the wealth we waste has never been in any sense ours. If this is not a national immorality and a social crime, I do not know what can be. Yesterday I was told about the purchase of twenty thousand acres of tall timber by a manufacturer of matches who, according to the account I have had of him, is not fit to be hanged from one of his own dead trees. While I write these words, a fire is raging in Idaho that has already destroyed a tract of forest as large as the state of Delaware. But this sort of thing, like automobile fatalities, is ceasing to be news. Demos yawns as he glances at the head-lines and turns to the comic strip.

Yet I think we may just pull through. In all parts of the country there are springing up agencies and enterprises, both public and private, for the protection of trees. In so far as these are unsentimental in their motives and educational in their methods, they are beneficent, and my sympathy goes out to

112

With Hatchet and Pruning Shears

them as heartily as it does to those who fight the gangster and the racketeer. They may win. In the meanwhile, here is my suggestion to them, which may have a superficial look of sentimentality but which is sound, I believe, at bottom. To every American child let there be given at birth, by the Forestry Department of the State in which he or she is born, one infant tree, to be cherished by him or her until death do them part. And then let us set aside Arbor Day, freeing it from every other kind of activity, as the day on which every man and woman and child in the land is expected to visit his tree and spend at least an hour with it, discovering what its needs are and providing for them at his or her own labor or expense, renewing acquaintance with this vegetable contemporary, this leafy twin.

An idle fancy, say you? I think not. The practical difficulties and expense are negligible. In the course of a year this plan would not cost the nation more than the unhanged match manufacturer, whom I have not named above, will spend in grinding his twenty thousand acres of forest into match-sticks. But what good would it do? For one thing, it would provide us with one more holiday, and we grievously need more. And then, no thoughtful person looking out at the modern scene can fail to realize that by far too many of us have lost all contact, all sense of kinship with the soil from which we come, to which we go. In America particularly we are an uprooted people. Hardly one adult American in a thousand lives now in the house where he was born. Loyalty and devotion to a few beloved acres, perhaps never very strong among us, is now all but utterly gone. Wealth, which we once clearly recognized as a child begotten upon the earth by human toil, now seems to most of us chiefly so much paper kept in the bank — or, when the bank fails, at least so much metal and rubber kept in the garage. I say that there is a serious question whether we can maintain human society, at least as we have hitherto known it, under these factitious and deracinated conditions. We have not been doing it very long, and we do not seem just at present to be doing it very well.

Now, a tree reminds us of several important things which most of us have forgotten — things we must recall without delay

The Cabin Down the Glen

if we are going on. (I know quite well the differences between men and trees are even more important than the similarities, but these are not the present theme.) There is something for us to admire, perhaps now and then to emulate, in the serenity with which a tree accepts whatever station fate has given it, making the best it can of whatever earth and light and air and rain it can get. The fact that a tree has only one foot is not pure misfortune; there are certain real compensations for this deficiency, and I suppose that millions of human beings would be wiser and more contented if they had been born monopodal too. A tree, moreover, knows perfectly well and never forgets where it's health and strength and very life come from. We have known, but we have forgotten. Trees never blaspheme the holy earth. In most of our religions and ethical systems, we do.

And so it seems to me that if my plan were adopted, there might be a good deal of profitable thinking going on during Arbor Day under the hundred and twenty million tree-twins of America. Certainly there would be such a growth of affection toward trees and such an increase in our sense of partnership with them, that the dastardly race of tree-butchers would very soon die out, not to be renewed. So would the sickly race of the sentimentalists, for everyone would then learn that both trees and human beings thrive the better by means of steady collaboration.

I shall not soon forget this morning's hour among the birches. The time and place were gay, as I have said, and so was I. One is always happy working among trees if he goes to save and not to destroy, but this particular task had a special charm. I allow a good deal for the splendor of the day. All the while I was up there I could hear the thrushes singing in the glen below. Two or three times there came, in the pauses of the wind, a fragment of the white-throat's whistle, that most magical of all sounds to be heard out-of-doors in America. And all morning long there was the great voice of the wind roaring from the northwest, dashing and clashing the branches over my head. Yet it was not the music of the day alone, nor the dancing of the daisies in the fields below, nor the sunshine

114

With Hatchet and Pruning Shears

spilling from every cloud and leaf and blade that made me also sing up there. Most of all, it was the sense I had of collaboration with a great partner in a necessary task. I knew that it was good for me to be there among the birches, and I knew that it was good for them to have me. A man was improving upon Nature, and Nature was improving upon a man.

TO BIRCHES IN LENT

Snow in your arms, sisters?
Snow at your feet?
Never a merry thought,
Never the beat
Of a dance or a song
All the day long?
Never a dream that darts
Forward, or echo caught
Out of the long ago
Summer? Deep at your very hearts
Nothing but snow?

Ah well, if I did not know you,
If I had never seen
The breath of the morning blow you
To chattering silver-green,
Or heard your gusts of laughter
And slow talk lisping after,
Or joined in the wild entrancing
Ecstasy of your dancing
Awry, down-bent, upheaved —
If we had not sung together
Through every change of weather,
I might have been deceived.

But now I think this thin disguise
Is for some other man's less loving eyes.
I know the gone and the coming sun
Burns at the hearts of you every one
Like love of God in a snow-white nun.

This is the poise of a dancer
Delaying a moment to answer
The throb of the stars and the rote of the
      rain and the penetrant pulse of the earth;
This is a deep breath taken
Before your song is shaken
Free on the wind to the hastening sky and
      over the land's green girth;
This is the thought that ranges
Under all times and changes
To bring us back from the roots of things
      their dance and their song and their mirth.

TINY JUNGLES

Lying face down in the tall grass, I have a view among the blue-green blades that extends for some three feet, but beyond that distance the grasses crowd so thickly together as to block every vista. Looking upward, I can see blue tatters and strips of sky between the taller blades. Higher still, three feet above my head, the heavily seeded and feathery grass tops are waving against a silvery cloud.

The eye soon grows accustomed to the change of scale and accepts inches in the place of yards, watching minute events as though they were great and stirring. That golden blur far off there on the edge of distance is really a buttercup, but there is no difficulty in imagining it a sunset. That disk of filmy white floating high among the tallest grasses might as well be a moon as a daisy. The stems of the grass itself look at first like trunks of enormously tall trees, perhaps of the eucalyptus kind, but they are too smooth and lustrous for that, and their enlarged joints make one think rather of masts of ships. They differ from trees also in their motion, for they rock and sway clear to their roots like masts when the wind goes by.

And yet this Lilliputian country is in other respects very like a jungle. Everywhere among the lower levels of the grass I see entanglement and disarray, the fresh green of this year's blades springing from the debris of years gone by. Here are ten thousand dead brown blades lying crisscross on the ground or lodged and leaning against the new growth or piled confusedly together in heaps and tussocks. As in the jungles of the Amazon or Congo, death and life are jostling here for room and are voraciously feeding one upon the other. The sun beats almost vertically down, but its rays do not pierce the deeper thickets. Millions of the lives brought forth here must be lived in shadow

Tiny Jungles

or in darkness. And lived, too, in the midst of what confusion! There seem to be no roads whatever through the wilderness — yet for the discovery of such things I shall do well not to trust the eyes of a foreigner, recently arrived. For aught I know the inhabitants find their way about as readily as we do through the streets of a city, and they may have many great thoroughfares leading from one center of population to another.

But are there any inhabitants? At first sight the jungle looks deserted. No traveler, no idler or sportsman even, is anywhere to be seen in the whole intricate landscape of shade and shine. Yet perhaps I should consider that those who may dwell here might be put off their beat for a moment by the sudden intrusion of a vast creature whose coming among them would be as though their sky was falling in. I wait for them to come out of hiding, take up their burdens, and go on their several journeys.

Almost immediately an inhabitant appears — or at least a piece of one. What name shall I put to that dim gray ghost, far in among the stems yonder, moving so stealthily about on so many long and slender legs, grasping each blade with a separate foot? A spider, no doubt; but an almost transparent, a certainly translucent spider — one who, like Plotinus, is ashamed of having any body whatever and has accordingly attenuated himself by strict ascetic discipline to the shadow of a shade. Or perhaps he has found "the receipt of a fern-seed" so that he can now walk invisible to birds and beetles. I am not quite sure that the grass blades on the other side of him show through his body, but I think they do. Yet frail as he looks, he has a most expeditious way of getting through tall timber, never touching the ground at all but walking on the sides of the trunks — and this, too, with such an amazing number of legs! To a mere biped it does not seem fair.

For a moment the phantasmal spider seems to have the whole jungle to himself, but when I look again, there are dozens and scores of denizens in full view, each of them practicing a different method of getting over the ground. The problem of locomotion and the struggle with space are primary here, and every inhabitant is exhibiting his private idea of a solution.

The Cabin Down the Glen

The most awkward of these, I should say, is that adopted by yonder inchworm, although he atones for his lack of grace in carriage by the beautiful silvery green of his coat. One cannot imagine how he ever thought up such a way of propelling himself as this endless touching of toes to head and then stretching out again, or why, having once thought of it, he did not instantly reject it as too ludicrous for public performance. Good for the spine no doubt it is, but it only makes me think of some highly ingenious method of mortifying the flesh worked out by a self-torturing Yogi. And yet the silver-green inchworm does make steady progress up the silver-green stem, not at all disturbed by the fact that he cuts a somewhat ridiculous figure. Indeed, there seems to be little painful self-consciousness in this country, little fear of making oneself conspicuous by oddities of dress, form, deportment, and gait. I see other inhabitants leaping from blade to blade across huge chasms, squirming along the ground, launching forth on wings, or swinging from lofty trapezes on ropes of silver. It is a land of go-as-you-please.

And most of these small people are singing or shouting aloud as they go, like "children of the King." Life celebrates its brief triumph in innumerable voices this July noon. Accustoming my ears to the fainter sounds, as I have my eyes to the smaller forms of the grass, I find it full of jubilation. Above the faint ticking and rasping of the grass blades themselves rises the stridor of a thousand crickets, and over that soars the long-drawn clamor of some great grasshopper, a sound that tears through the jungle like the mort blown by Roland in the Pass of Ronceveaux so that Charlemagne heard it two hundred miles away.

A circle three feet in diameter, counting out the large segment covered by my body, is all that I see of the jungle, but within that area at this moment there must be a thousand creatures fair or monstrous, crawling or creeping, walking or running or leaping or flying, each of them with some kind of importance to itself and perhaps (how do I know?) to others, each of them cherishing some faint spark of vitality and cunningly handing it on across the generations. Ah, the terror, the unspeakable pathos, of life! All at once while I gaze down

Tiny Jungles

into these few sunny handsbreadths, there comes to me a flashing image of the vast oceans of the grass billowing and surging over the planet, a vision of the prairies and steppes and pampas and llanos and savannas, all teeming with myriads of lives, most of them far more prolific of forms than this small patch of Connecticut. The mystery of life's profusion and wastefulness is as insoluble here as it is when we think of our own crowded cities, and the wars and plagues and famines that periodically drain away their superfluous millions.

But I know so little about the small people of the grass that it would be as well to admit a complete ignorance. What hopes and aspirations are theirs, what thoughts they have, what sorrows, and what satisfactions as the reward of toil, I can guess no more than I can the secrets of the farthest star. Knowing nothing about them, we tend to ignore their existence and to consider them of no importance; but they are older by far than we men, and they have solved the problems of their condition so much better than we have ours as to make it seem probable to some observers that they will see us all to bed. I have come too recently from the jungles of the upper world, which also I do not understand, to see much meaning in this one. The best that I can do is to single out an individual here and there from the mass of these strange creatures and to endow that one with purposes and feelings somewhat like my own — a process as inevitable as it is fallacious.

I select, for example, a very small red ant that has been climbing at a great speed up one of the smaller blades of grass and has now reached the very pinnacle. There he stands alone in the wash of empty space, with nothing but blue sky between him and Arcturus. I should say, to be generous, that he measures one eighth of an inch in length, and in that case the height on which he stands corresponds to some eight hundred feet for a human being — a height at which I, at least, should begin to feel somewhat giddy if I were so slenderly supported as he is and swinging so wildly and helplessly about in the sky. But the little red ant is apparently a steeple-jack of long experience. He is alternately rubbing his hands

The Cabin Down the Glen

together and gesticulating like the foreman of a surveying party. Or perhaps he is a scout sent up by an army to spy out the land, and all this waving of fore-legs and antennae may belong to some elaborate set of military signals. Or else he may be a sun worshipper pouring forth his soul in prayer and this tall blade his minaret.

Or I pass for a moment into this adventurous spider, somewhat larger than the head of a pin, who has become thoroughly disgusted with the labor of toiling through thickets of underbrush. Finding himself pressed for time, he has ascended a grass blade to a height of three inches and is now meditating a magnificent leap to a blade almost an inch and a half away. (And yet why leap to that other blade? Why cannot he be content with the one on which he now stands, seeing that it gets as much sunlight and is in every way as eligible as the other, and seeing too that if ever he reaches the second blade a third will then loom beyond it as the goal of all ambition? But in asking that question, I touch one of the central mysteries of life common to men and spiders, and in order to answer it I should have to look down upon both species equally.)

I consider the abyss that yawns below him and the great distance he hopes to cross — some sixty feet if the leap were mine. Well may he pause for repeated consideration and measuring of his strength against that chasm! He advances to the very brink, prepares to jump — and then draws back. Perhaps some fleeting picture has crossed his brain of the ruin that would result from failure, of the shattered limbs and other *disjecta membra* [scattered members/limbs] of a spider that would flutter down the void. Who can blame him if it be so? Certainly not I. But perhaps there are admiring eyes below there which he dares not disappoint. More potent still, there may be onlookers who have warned him against this hazardous attempt or have declared that no spider of his size can ever perform such a feat! Whatever the urgency that impels him, it drives him once more to the edge of the blade and forces him to survey again that dizzy gap. His brain whirls at the sight and his heart sickens. He recoils. He lies ignominiously

Tiny Jungles

down in the valley of the grass blade and pretends to forget his reason for coming there.

By this time the sporting instinct awakes in me and I take my stand among the spectators on the ground. I imagine the glory that would follow success, and my heart thrills at the splendor of the leap as a billion hearts throughout the world were thrilling not long ago when a lonely man with a kitten in his pocket leapt the Atlantic from New York to Paris. "Ah, come now!" I say to the speck of life on the grass blade before me, knowing well that it is not really asleep. "What is life and limb in comparison with such fame as may be yours? Consider the terrible ignominy of defeat, which only death can cancel. Think, too, of the possible contribution to science.

> *He either fears his fate too much*
> *Or his deserts are small,*
> *That dares not put it to the touch*
> *To gain or lose it all."*

And now at last, whether roused by my own words or by those ringing lines from the Marquis of Montrose, the tiny hero bestirs himself with a new determination. Once more he marches boldly to the edge of the void with his teeth — if he has any — firmly set; once more he gathers the might of every limb — and he has many — into one compact bundle beneath him. And then, though his head whirls and every instinct but one rebels against the attempt, he launches himself like a leaping tiger into empty space.

Will he reach the other side? No. Ah, no! The thing is impossible. But yes! He has reached it! One tenacious claw has caught the saw-toothed edge of the blade at which he aimed himself, and by this claw alone he drags his whole weight up to safety. And now, having perhaps won for himself a sempiternity of fame, or at any rate having saved a good hour of labor by an audacious short cut, he indulges himself in an hour's nap in the sun.

But hark! Was that a tiny cheer from the watchers below?

RURAL FREE DELIVERY

There are not many men with whom I would willingly exchange occupations, even for a short while. As I run through the list of the professions, businesses, crafts, arts, trades, sports, leisures, and idlings, each of which has of course its own charm and advantages for those who know it best, I remain modestly content with my own lot and my own kind of work. If it is somewhat more arduous than most others, my easy solution is to engage in it with more ardor. Only when I hear the familiar blast of a horn from up the road in the morning and go forth with my bundle of letters to chat with R.F.D., do I feel some momentary doubts. I would not say that he has chosen more wisely or luckily than I have, but it is clear that he also has things about right. He also works hard, though not for such long hours as mine, but he enjoys every minute of his work and turns it into a kind of play.

This R.F.D. travels through forty miles of Connecticut landscape on every weekday, and that amounts to twelve thousand five hundred miles — or half-way round the world — in every year. Seasons and weathers never deter him. He likes them all equally well. In winter, riding a world all white, he has to cut his way through the drifts of the river road; and six months later the lush and fronded wealth of midsummer impedes his progress almost as much by the drifts that have turned to green. He hears the first faint stir of spring and sees the earliest bluebird flash from the fence rail to the bare apple bough. Best of all, he has nothing to do in October but to ride where the gold and the scarlet are boldest. How he can refrain, at that season, from leaving a letter now and then for some flaming maple or dogwood — so much more vivid than any of the people on his route — I fail to understand. Perhaps he does

Rural Free Delivery

not always check the impulse. A few of the letters I have vainly looked for may have gone that way.

Yes, he has things about right, this wise and lucky R.F.D.; and he knows it, too. He has counted his many blessings. His cup is almost visibly running over. He is the kind of man, like Falstaff and Chaucer's Monk and Mr. Pickwick, that it does one good just to think about. When I am falling asleep at night I like to follow him in fancy as he threads his forty miles of Connecticut's October, gleaning and garnering every tint against the months of frost. Nothing escapes him. Not a fringed or a closed gentian in the deepest shadow of his road blooms in vain. He sees how the asters come and go — the little asters and the large, the white and the blue, those that hang heavy on thick bending stems and those that are like a mist on the hillside. Goldenrod in shadow, he sees, is a different and a far older gold than the goldenrod in sunshine. He watches the chromatic progressions of the woods and observes the overnight changes of every larger tree. He could tell you that the woodbine on such an old gray stone wall is dropping rubies now, that the elms of such a village green are red-brown like a ploughed field, and that the sugar maples in Farmer Clarke's wood lot will reach their height of color tomorrow morning. The landscape opens out a little more for him each day, showing vistas half forgotten because unseen for half a year. As he goes down the river road, the golden leaves keep pace with him, floating on the water. Restless little companies of migrants, gathered kind by kind for their long flight, flutter up from the thicket at his approach and settle quickly back again when they find that it is only he. I can hear him rumbling over bridges in quiet hollows where the sound of his coming precedes him by a mile so that a short letter can be commenced and finished before he is at the door. I hear him bumping cheerfully down our hill roads — certainly among the worst and the most charming roads of all the world — and chugging determinedly up again, shouting to men in the fields, chaffing with boys and girls, tossing a friendly word to every wayside dog. On some of the lanes he traverses — my own, I am glad to say, included — he is usually the only

The Cabin Down the Glen

man who passes all day long; but he brings more humanity into them than is to be found in many a city street.

Cheerfulness and a keen eye for all the color and form and motion of the road are what might reasonably be expected of a man with his advantages. Who, indeed, would not be cheerful if he could spend most of his waking time riding about among the trees? But the people along his route are more to R.F.D. than the trees are, and he studies them more closely. Almost everything of an out-of-door nature that happens on his forty miles of road, or near it, he knows about and is glad to tell you. Farmer Johnson is blasting stumps this week — a fact which explains the dull detonations that one has been hearing in the southwest — and hopes to get his upper pasture clear before snow flies. Farmer Edwards has just taken a second crop of hay from that fine meadow of his in the brook bottom. Mrs. Ledyard up by the mill has finished her fall canning and has gone to Salisbury to visit relatives for a week. Mrs. Sampson, the preacher's wife, has had another baby, a boy. Such seeds of information he strews broadcast up and down the road — but never, even if he collects them, any tales of malicious gossip.

In this and in several other ways R.F.D. takes the place of the tinkers and peddlers who used to come among these hills two or three times a year instead of once a day, carrying almost the only news of the outer world that many lonely people had. Considering that he brings our newspapers and books and magazines as well as our letters, he is by all odds our chief link with the world at large, and he supplements the news from beyond the farther horizons with many a local item which strangers would care nothing about. For the whole various district of up-and-down and in-and-out to be seen from the top of my highest hill, he is the chief intelligencer, the brief abstract and chronicle, the Mercury in a Ford car.

Hardly anyone I know has a wider circle of acquaintance than R.F.D., whether in numbers or in social and intellectual range. He knows the German immigrant who is still bravely struggling to pronounce "th" and also the family whose title to

Rural Free Delivery

their land is said to go back to King Charles the First. He, and he only, calls upon the hermit in his hut by the river and also upon the New York millionaire in his palace on the hill. At one stop he chats with the farmer's wife who has never learned to read at all, and at the next he talks with the scholar who has read altogether too much. He hears what each of these people has to say and then drives on — ruminating, comparing, contrasting, drawing cautious conclusions about this and that way of life, and finally concluding, I hope, that it is best of all to be R.F.D.

While the years pass, he sees all these people changing. They change more slowly than the trees do in spring and autumn, but still they change, and he has been driving this route for so long now that he can draw wide comparisons. He compares Farmer Johnson not only with other farmers but with himself and sees that he is not quite the same man that he was ten years ago. He observes how the quantity of mail delivered at one farm falls off and how it increases at another. Farmer Brown has not heard from his only son in the city, he knows, for several months. At last a letter does come, and Brown reads it aloud to him while resting one foot on the running board, just to prove that he is not forgotten after all. Farmer Brown is more pleased by that letter than R.F.D. likes to see.

On some days my mail arrives at nine o'clock in the morning, but that is only when no housewife has asked R.F.D. to shift a stovepipe or to take a look at the water heater and when no farmer on the first stretch of his road has enlisted his help in lifting a heavy rock out of a field. Other days I do not hear his horn until nearly noon, and then there is no telling how many trades and professions he has dipped briefly into since he finished his breakfast. For there seems to be hardly any limit to the number of different things that a handy and willing R.F.D. may be asked to do as he rides about the countryside, with no particular duties except covering forty miles of bad road and delivering mail at three or four hundred houses. Everywhere he arrives he is an extra man, a very present help, and a friend.

127

The Cabin Down the Glen

When I first became acquainted with R.F.D., I decided that he must be not only omnilaborious but omnivorous as well. It was simply amazing to me to consider the number and the quantity of things he could eat — or that he would carry away, at any rate, with a promise to eat them. Very soon I gave up asking him whether he liked apples, pears, peaches, melons, squashes, onions, radishes, sweet corn, grapes, pie, cake, doughnuts, bread, and so on; it grew clear that nothing edible came amiss to him, so that I simply carried out whatever extra viands I had in the cabin and watched them roll away.

But after a while I learned, partly by observation and then by direct inquiry, that he was not necessarily such a phenomenal trencherman as I had supposed, the fact being that he is the father of nine children, no less. The mystery was somewhat clarified, and yet I was left wondering, quite as much as I did before, at the man's huge affection for the human race. To me, with the silence and solitude of twenty-five wild acres wrapped about me, there was something that overwhelmed the fancy in the mere thought of R.F.D.'s uproarious home. And from that home, I knew, "still soul-hydroptic with a sacred thirst," he must needs dart daily forth and positively splash and bathe himself in the warm-flowing stream of humanity! One of these nine children he always carries with him every day when school is not in session; but even at that, of course, it takes him a week and a half to get round the list, so that by the time he begins on the second lap one gets the names and faces of the smaller R.F.D.'s. confused and has to ask, "Which is this one?" Not that it matters greatly, for they are all of them bright-eyed, quick-witted youngsters, wise beyond their years in the varieties and vagaries of human nature. Travel has made them so. In spite of the best eremitic intentions, I find that I get interested in these children, as I am interested also in their father and in all the men and women up and down the road that he tells me about. The fact is that there is not much use in trying to be an orthodox hermit on the route of such a wise, happy, philanthropic, and philoprogenitive R.F.D.

PATERNITY

Considering how nobly my hills are clothed by trees of other kinds, I was at first a little surprised, and not a little disappointed, to find them so deficient in oaks. But now I know the explanation. Half a mile down the lane, at the meeting of the two rivers that almost surround me, I have discovered the ruins of an old forge where cannon were founded for the War of the Revolution. Many of the oaks that might otherwise be about me were sacrificed on what is called "the altar of patriotism," which is in some ways very like the altar of Moloch. Properly to slay young men it has always been found necessary to slay trees. And two miles across the valley stands a house in which, more than a hundred years ago, there flourished a domestic manufacture of wooden dolls. Up to that house went many other oaks that might have been mine, destined to be wheeled about in small carriages, to be rocked in tiny cradles all through these eastern states, and to be given an even warmer affection than I should have shown them by girls who have long been dust. Thus they did their share in the blind and wasteful hurly-burly of life, helping as much to deepen the maternal instinct in the future mothers of New England as they did to kill the sons of English mothers. Perhaps I should not begrudge them.

The result is, however, that I have few oaks of really quercine height and girth with that good crooked mightiness and color of green rust which only a century can produce. This is a deprivation. Hemlocks, birches, beeches, pines are well enough in their way, but their way is so predominantly feminine that I often ask myself, as I go about my land, the same subconscious question that one asks in American society: "Where are all the men?" Nothing takes the place of an old oak's solid dependable power. No other tree grips the earth with such huge knees or

The Cabin Down the Glen

fights the storm wind with such a hundred arms or looks so much at home with its head among the stars. An old oak is a warrior and a philosopher at once, like Socrates. He helps one to keep in mind that beauty is also masculine; and yet not by his beauty so much as by sheer might and ancientness of days he spreads around him a religious awe. He shows that this is after all a tragic world, coextensive with the reaches of our souls, and that majesty has not yet forsaken it. Therefore I have a need of oaks, as deep as the need of those faraway children for wooden dolls and almost as strong as the need of those English lads for death. Well, then, I must plant them.

I choose a day of early spring with the west wind breathing and go forth armed with an iron dibble. My pockets are bulging with acorns. Many of them were gathered last autumn along the neighboring lanes and in the glades near at hand. Whenever I saw a good oak I scuffled and raked among the leaves at his feet until I had gathered all the seed of him that I could find, and these I brought home and kept moist during the winter. Others come from the shores of Walden Pond, so that children of the oaks that talked to Emerson and Thoreau may someday whisper here. Others still I have brought from England, where the grandest of all oak trees grow, and from the Catskills, and from a tree in southern Connecticut that shades a house I love. Over my shoulder hangs a heavy sack of acorns gathered for me by the son of a friend of mine on the other side of the River of New England.

Here, then, is God's plenty of acorns. As I plunge my hand among them, they give me a thrilling sense of power. Each one is a tiny bomb with a very long time fuse — so long, in fact, that its explosion will scarcely be completed in less than a hundred years — and I am an anarchist plotting wreck and ruin to the realm of ugliness, a conspirator going forth to perpetrate beauty. "Have a care, now," I say. "Look out for yourselves, you tree butchers, realtors, planters of billboards, grabbers of water-

Paternity

power, filthy politicians, and vulgarians all and sundry who can feel comfortable only in a land laid as bare as your souls! For what is all your strength compared with that of an acorn? What hold have you on time, or what help from the Nature of Things? I am carrying enough oak seeds here to cover the continent with one 'boundless continuity of shade' — and how will you feel then? There is enough nobility in this one sack to wither you and your kind forever." — But all of this, I reflect, although it is a consummation devoutly to be wished, will take a good deal of time, and time is precisely what one should resolve to think as little as possible about while planting oaks.

If anything adequate has ever been written in praise of acorns, I have not seen it. They deserve a place in that famous catalogue, drawn up by Marcus Aurelius in his *Golden Book*, of things delightful merely "because they happen naturally," such as "the hanging downe of grapes, the browe of a Lyon, the froathe of a foaming wilde boare." How firm they are, how packed with the future, these potential parents of forests! I take one from my pocket, hold it in my hand, toss it, gaze at it, striving to realize that in this small brown case lies coiled and sleeping all the character and habit of an oak. The shape of the leaves, the color of the bark, the girth and strength and texture of the boughs that are to be — all are implicit here. I try to comprehend that a huge and intricate tree has managed to crowd its essential self into this compass so as to cross the gulf of winter and hide from the eyes of Death. Is it not as though we should be able to deduce from one of the sonnets of Shakespeare the color of his eyes, the shape of his hand, the tones of his voice, his very gait and gesture, and why women loved him? O, I think that when a man has pondered long and deeply enough on the mystery of acorns, he will scarcely find anything else too hard to believe. Go to the oak, thou atheist!

From the mere look and taste and texture of these seeds I could tell that they came from a strong, stubborn tree. They are all intensely oaken, yet each bears the mark of kind. Consider their many shapes and hues and sizes, their different ways of bulging from their cups or of lying all but hidden within, their

The Cabin Down the Glen

angles on the twigs, their weights with relation to bulk. I need not study the textbooks in order to know the seed of the white oak at a glance from those of the red and the black. Nine times out of ten I can select it from a jumble of others by the sense of touch alone, and I am told that some men can distinguish acorns by the sense of taste. Surely this idiosyncrasy of theirs, so sharply defined and pervasive, is one reason for their charm, and the pleasure I take in them is somewhat like that of Chaucer in all things and persons abounding in their own kind. I think there is something in the very word "acorn" — something old and tough and honest and right — as oaken as a word can be. I am glad that it is not a pretty word, a lady's word, and that it means just what it says, "oak-seed." Ladies, male and female, think about seeds as little as possible. Instinctively they realize that the topic is tabu — that is, holy — and one for timorous and shallow minds to avoid.

But now comes the question, where to plant. Ought my oaks of the future to stand in orderly rows or be scattered here and there to make a glade? Should they loom along the skyline or fill the hollows? Should they rise among other trees or separately? These are problems, harder than I foresaw. I had thought to drop seeds at haphazard, almost, into every space between the laurels where the young trees would get enough light; but now I find that I must try to imagine how these acres will be looking, or ought to look, at least a century hence. That is not easy. The great pine yonder by the cabin will be gone then, for it has already reached the limit of its growth. Should an oak fill the space that will be left in the sky, or may I provide for a better vista by doing nothing to fill that future gap?

Thus I find that a man cannot even plant oaks on his "own land" while thinking of himself alone. This brown seed between my thumb and finger, so small and light that a jay could easily carry it off in his bill, may well make a huge difference to eyes that will never meet mine — to the eyes, perhaps, of my great-great-grandson, whose taste in such matters I cannot possibly guess. By his time, for aught I know, America may have gone in for geometrical and formal gardening, so that

Paternity

everything I do this afternoon will be a cause of aesthetic offense, like the planting done in England two centuries ago by "Capability Brown."

But why should I bother my head about this possible descendent of mine who has not even been born? Well, I do. The oak trees in my pocket have not been born either. They are his, not mine. I should plant a birch tree to suit my own taste, but oaks I plant for him. It is the landscape of the future that I am shaping this afternoon, and I care more for that future landscape which I shall never see than I do for the one actually before me. And so, with a considerable sense of responsibility, I wander up and down for half an hour, faltering and hesitant, piercing the sod here and there with the dibble but always thinking better of it and moving on without planting a single seed.

Ah, the future! Why can it not let us alone? As if we had not enough on hand to learn a little about the past and hold what was good in it while shaping a course through the sufficiently bewildering present! Yet it will give us no peace. In exact ratio to the degree of humanity that we attain comes the realization that we are tenants at will on a lease the only certain thing in which is that it is very brief and that we are profoundly responsible to and for those who shall come after. The criminal and the dullard may ignore this, but only such as they.

At last I find a ridge of land where any eyes that care at all for trees will certainly be glad, forever, to see a range of oaks. In goes the dibble, and I plant my first acorn half an inch below the surface. "Grow tall and strong and fatherly," I say to it as I draw the earth gently back and rearrange the grasses to deceive the squirrels. Then I move on for some fifty feet, for oaks need plenty of room, and plant another. All along that ridge I plant them, and then along a second ridge, and a third, until, near the close of the afternoon, I have set out perhaps two hundred oak seeds. I do not pretend, even to myself, that it has been skillfully done. The scientific way, I believe, would have been to start the trees in wet sand under glass and then to transplant them; but it is enough to say that I should not

The Cabin Down the Glen

have enjoyed that. Hoping thereby to atone for all deficiencies of method, I give them a general blessing — something out of Genesis about multiplying and replenishing the earth — and then I find a seat in the late sunshine and rest. It has been a good day. Few men in America have made a stronger mark on the future this day than I have made. Great-great-grandson of mine, I hope you will like the result!

While I am sitting there on a fallen log in a brown study, time, for once, is good to me. It draws aside the curtain. As though in a moving picture enormously speeded up so that centuries flash by in minutes, I see the oaks of the future leap from the sod and shoot skyward, exploding into numberless boughs and billions of leaves. In less time than I take to tell it, they grow huge and old as Cowper's Yardley Oak, planted by the daughter of William the Conqueror —

> *giant bulks*
> *Of girth enormous, with moss-cushioned root*
> *Upheav'd above the soil, and sides emboss'd*
> *With prominent wens globose.*

They cast a mile-long shadow down these hills at dawn and evening, and lovers of great trees come from far to see them, as I have gone to Sherwood and the Forest of Dean, to Waverly in Massachusetts and to North Ashford and Rattlesnake Mountain in Connecticut. Six, eight, ten, twelve hundred years fleet by, and still they stand, they or their children, the survivors filling in the gaps made by the north wind. Fourteen, fifteen, sixteen hundred years, and yet they have not reached the age of the Oak of Cowthorpe or the "Grette Oake" near Shrewsbury where Owen Glendower took refuge five centuries ago. Seventeen, eighteen, nineteen hundred years, and even then they are younger than the Oak of Damorey in Dorsetshire, whose hollow trunk sheltered an ale house in the days of the Commonwealth. There must be many oaks now flourishing in the world that were born before the birth of Christ; I myself know two or three in Connecticut

Paternity

that go back to the time of Chaucer; and I can see no reason why some that I have planted this afternoon should not have an equal longevity.

Ah, but I shall never see them with any but the eyes of fancy! They will spring from the soil just as I am sinking back into it, and the rhythms of their lives will be very different from that of mine. Although their thin white rootlets will soon be groping down into land called mine, their crowns will rise and spread in a time not mine at all — in a world to me unknown, unimaginable. If I am to have any part or lot in that world, these oaks are likely to be my sole representatives. That being so, there is a mystery in my occupation of this afternoon and in the pleasure it gave me, which is connected with some of the deeper things in our human nature.

For I did take a keen pleasure in gathering these acorns and in planting them here. But a pleasure of what kind? What was the impulse that sent forth "Johnny Appleseed" and kept him wandering for fifty years in the wake of the covered wagons, always moving westward and always planting trees as he went? His raiment was a gunny sack, his hat was a stew pan, he walked barefooted in all seasons, he fed on berries, he usually slept where night found him, and he died in his sleep on a farmer's kitchen floor after having recited the Beatitudes to pay for his night's lodging. (To think of his having said that very night these very words: "Blessed are the meek, for they shall inherit the earth"!) Long before the death of this half-legendary American saint, it was estimated that the trees he had planted would shade a hundred thousand square miles of America. You may find them today far out on the western prairies, although the man who planted them came from New England. Also you may find their children and their children's children, although Johnny Appleseed left no child of his own flesh. I suggest that there is something here not sufficiently accounted for by those philosophers who assert that we never do anything without a selfish motive.

"Who planteth a vineyard and eateth not the fruit thereof?" angrily asks the Apostle Paul in his first letter to the Christians

The Cabin Down the Glen

of Corinth. The question is rhetorical, intended to imply that no
man is such a fool. As a matter of fact, we all do precisely this
sort of thing just insofar as we are human, and this is one of
the most interesting and extenuating traits that an impartial
observer would find in us. The ancient poet Statius, wise in
this regard and more truly Christian than Paul, remarks it as
one of the mysteries of our nature than an old man should
take pleasure in setting out trees which only the following
ages can enjoy. Cicero twice refers to this passage, once in the
essay "On Old Age" and, more thoughtfully, in the *Tusculan
Disputations*, where he declares that the man who plants
a slowly growing tree must have in mind the great human
society which never dies and must feel that he belongs to it.
He observes, also, what is sufficiently evident, that this action
is a fair type or symbol of the selfless work done by the lawgiver,
the statesman, the scholar, and the father. Yes, the father.
In that hint he comes nearest to my experience. In this planting
of seeds that are to take hold on the ages, there has been a
vague sense of paternity.

Certainly I do not mean to imply any conscious and deliberate
altruism on my part. I am not like those Victorian fathers who
strove to give their sons the impression that they had been
begotten as a personal favor and at a considerable personal
sacrifice. Nature has to bribe us to some of our best actions,
and it is often the part of honesty to "take the cash and let the
credit go." Freely I admit that I have enjoyed my tree planting
this afternoon and also that I did it because I liked to; but
this admission does not destroy the higher values, the deeper
significances, the under-and-over-tones of the act. For my part,
I reject with a kind of loathing the contemporary view that the
lowest interpretation to be put upon any piece of conduct is
always the true and complete one. The truth about every act,
however simple in appearance, is always, to a thinking mind,
complex beyond all finding out. Consider the simplest act of all,
the sexual. At one extreme it eludes us in the darkness of the
flesh, and at the other it outsoars us into a blinding holiness.
And just as we owe far more to this simple yet incomprehensible

Paternity

act than either beasts or prudes will ever guess, just as we have
built upon and deduced from it numberless intricate structures
of art and manners and morals, so I think we may owe something to the simple act of planting trees, its analogue. Indeed, it
seems not impossible that the august conception of humanity
at large, of the deathless human society, *commune humanitatis
corpus* [the common/shared body of humanity], which Cicero
was one of the first to seize and express, was hinted by the
very question I am now asking: for whom does one plant the
trees he will never enjoy? Francis Petrarch suggests a religious
significance in such planting, and I should hesitate to say that
he is wrong. Certainly there is a triumph in it, however brief,
over all personal considerations and interests. It exhilarates
and enlarges and liberates the spirit because it is done from
something, call it what we may, which is not ourselves — for
something that stretches out and beyond us on every side,
for something eternal of which we are and have been and shall
be forever a part.

But now the light is fading on the hill. The seeds I have
planted lie snug in the warm fertile flesh of the earth. I leave
them to the darkness and the ages.

Good night! Good night! *Moriturus vos saluto.* [I who am
about to die salute you all.]

THANKSGIVING

(As written by the Hermit in the Cabin Down the Glen in the Year of Our Lord 3000)

For these great oaks that wall my hills about
    And guard the holy secret of the glen,
I give my thanks to one long blotted out
    Of every other record known to men.

When twilight takes them, or when early dawn
    Reveals them slowly emerging from the gloom,
I think that not quite all of him has gone
    Back to the dust in his forgotten tomb.

When they are standing black in the sunset's gold,
    When moonlight washes every glimmering stem,
But most of all when they have stars to hold,
    My thoughts return to him who fathered them.

Oh, was he granted one prophetic hour
    Before the coming on of his long night,
One vision or dream of their majestic power
    And the glory of their hundred-armed might?

They have the strength that he could never gain;
    They have the beauty he could only seek;
They learn in peace what he found out in pain;
    They sing serenely what he could not speak.

For they are rooted in the source of things;
    Their boughs are gashed with honorable scars;
They are the haven of many wandering wings;
    Their crowns are old familiars of the stars.

Yet surely something of him must endure
    In these, his children, that time cannot destroy;
As they are strong, his love of earth was pure;
    As they are fair, his heart was filled with joy.

    Who walks in the pearly eve and the pale dawn here
    Under the rustling of his million leaves? —
His leaves, that say and sing: "Far happier
    Is he who gives than he who but receives.

THE STONES OF THE PLACE

The table at which I now sit writing is not like other tables. For one thing, it weighs a good five hundred pounds, and it is made of solid granite. Two great dray horses dragged it here on a stone boat from one of my boundary walls, and five strong men lifted it into place on its pedestal of rock. Standing now under the hemlock beside my huge open fireplace, also of stone, it is ready for a banquet of Gargantua. Excavators, ages hence, digging down to these vast remains, will say to one another, "There were giants in those days!"

When my friends boast of their antique furniture, I smile the smile invisible. King Arthur's Round Table, now hanging on the wall of Winchester Castle, is recent in comparison with mine; and the dining table shown in a London Inn of Court, carved from the oaken timbers of the Spanish Armada, is a trinket of yesterday. My table too is part of a ship, but of one far older than Noah's Ark. It is taken from the timbers of this "vast tellurian galleon" on which we sail the sky.

A satisfactory thing about rocks and stones is that they do not soon wear out so that each may play in its time a good many parts; but I imagine that this leaf of granite before me has had as strange a career or, at any rate, as remarkable a culmination — I call it that — as most. To lie for millions of years in the dark under enormous pressure; to be lifted on the shoulders of the earthquake while the green seas slid away; to bask in the sun for other millions of years, gathering moss and lichens, making friends with the frost and the storm wind; to be lifted again, with numberless others, by a huge southbound glacier that moves a few feet in a year — what a lumbering, almighty stone boat was that! — and then to be melted out, dumped on a foreign hill, split by the chisel of frost into a wafer six inches thick and five

The Stones of the Place

feet square, dragged to a stone wall to lie for a century or two, and, finally, to be dug out again with pickaxes and crow-bars, hoisted on another stone boat, dragged over the hills, balanced on other rocks to make a table top and to have an essay written literally upon it! There is versatility.

Another charm that I find in these old bones of the planet is that I can fancy them whatever I please and no one can prove me wrong — unless it be some pedantic killjoy with a geologist's hammer, and to that sort of person I pay not the slightest heed. Ah, the blessings of ignorance! Imagination has a wide free field to wander in as I stand by the old wall poking this and that stone with my walking stick, dreaming out its biography. Only one thing I can be sure of concerning these great round wayworn fellows: they come from a long way off in space and time. Like me, they are really vagabonds, settling down for a while to think things out, and before long they will have to be on the move again. If I should say that some are ungerminated kernels of the stone seeds that Deucalion and Pyrrha threw over their shoulders to renew the human race, the conjecture would be my privilege. If I wish to think that I have here the very boulder that Polyphemus heaved and hurled after Odysseus, making a resounding splash in the Mediterranean, who shall prevent me? Now and then I find in the wall a great black stone like a tremendous cinder, which I choose to believe has whirled and drifted for eons in the sky so that now I may take the very falling star which gave us the legend of Prometheus the Fire-Bringer and use it for my hearthstone. And what was that smooth round bit of quartz that I found yesterday and brought home in my pocket, so fine it was in texture and white as new snow? Perhaps the pebble that killed Goliath. Or again, if this table top were the very rock once lying half asleep in the sun on Ararat upon which Noah first stepped forth, stranger things than that might be found in the walls of New England. For my part, although I know that some questionable authorities claim it for England's Coronation Chair, I should not be surprised to find in my wall that "one of the stones of the place" which Jacob put under his head as the base of

The Cabin Down the Glen

the ladder of glory seen in his dream, with the angels of God ascending and descending on it.

I like that old inexhaustible legend. For me it signifies, among other things, that the highest dreams often stoop to the hardest pillows. It suggests a consanguinity which I have often suspected between the stones of the field and the stars in their courses. I like to remember, also, that Jacob did not apparently spend much time in selecting his stone. He did not insist, for example, upon its being a diamond. Were they not all holy and so all good enough to dream on? Therefore he took the first that came to hand. But when he awoke and saw that this was the gate of heaven, "he took the stone that he had put under his head and set it up for a pillar and poured oil upon the top of it" and declared it to be the house of God.

Jacob got that good idea out of Egypt, where most of our religious ideas began and where men used to think more respectfully of stones than they ever have elsewhere — except, perhaps, in Connecticut. For at least a thousand years before Jacob's time the dreamers beside the Nile had been convinced that a departed spirit could be married to a stone if only one knew the right ceremonial notes to blow on the sacred trumpet so that the two would become, as it were, one flesh. They held, also, that the gods themselves often took up lodgings in stones and that by the proper anointings one could induce them to do so somewhat as a beekeeper handles a swarm. These entirely natural convictions were spread throughout the western world before recorded history began, going wherever the thoughts and dreams of Egypt went — and where did they not go? We find the trace of them in the standing stones of Crete and Mycenae, of South Africa and the Hebrides, as well as in thousands of menhirs, dolmens, comlechs, and cairns scattered throughout western Europe. We may yet discover it in Mexico and Yucatan and among the American Indians.

What sufficient motive can there have been for this almost worldwide collecting of great stones — of this lithomania, as it seems to us, that was epidemic among early mankind? I have spent a day among the fallen and tottering giants of Avebury

The Stones of the Place

Circle, that tremendous work which makes Stonehenge look like child's play, and I know that the men of old did not gather the five hundred "Sarsens" that originally composed it — some of them weighing nearly a hundred tons — for pure amusement. Neither was it for physical exercise that someone, three or four thousand years ago, brought from a distance and set on end the monolith of Morbihan in Brittany, sixty-seven feet long and weighing about three hundred and fifty tons. I can remember the time when any half-educated mind confronted with this problem would murmur the blessed word "phallicism," letting it go at that; and, indeed, considering what we know about lingam stones and the like, there may be something in the suggestion. But by whatever subsidiary name we may call it, the motive cannot have been anything less than religious. Stonehenge, Carnac, the Rollright Stones, and Avebury were in some sense temples, built by men who felt that every great rock contains a god. It was before the gods, invisible within or upon the mighty stones, that they danced and sang and feasted in the cirque on Salisbury Plain and that greater one on Marlborough Downs. If one were to be tried, where could he expect better justice? If he were to die under the sacrificial knife, where could he die more gladly or with a more certain reward? In the little pits of the outer circle at Stonehenge, a large number of human bones have recently been unearthed. Oh, well, we still sacrifice young men to gold. Why not to granite? Thither came the sick and the crippled, the insane and the barren, the unlucky and the dead, to be made whole. Does anyone doubt that they were so? Not I. And neither do I doubt that the custom attributed to the "Druids" of making their patients and neophytes sleep on stone pillows would still be highly effective.

This old adoration of stones is almost gone now, together with most other kinds of adoration. Somewhat amusingly, but with an unconscious pathos, we now tend to call it "idolatry." And what if it was? What if an idol, in the strict sense, was only the result of a little carving to bring out the lines of the god whose presence in the stone nobody doubted — a slight concession to the weakness of the eye of faith, a lifting of the stony veil to show

143

The Cabin Down the Glen

the divinity already there? After all, there is something to be said for the idols — something which the ancient Hebrew prophets and modern missionaries seem not to have considered. They do pin the gods down to one place, it is true; but then there are all the attendant advantages of knowing where to find those gods. Correspondingly, there are certain disadvantages in letting the gods loose, for once you have decided that they are "everywhere," you are next door to the sad conviction that they are nowhere.

Perhaps, however, this old feeling for stones is not entirely lost. Why is it that we still continue the use of headstones at our graves, ugly and expensive and unnecessary as they are? To perpetuate our names, I am told; but a marker of lead would do that as well and for a longer time. To "implore the passing tribute of a sigh," says Thomas Gray; but I do not find myself sighing in graveyards anymore than I do elsewhere. In fact, I find those of New England rather hilarious places. And here is a strange fact, hard to account for according to the ordinary notion of headstones: less than a mile from me at this moment there is an old graveyard crowded with rough-hewn stones upon which there is not now and there has never been a single name or date or other inscription. Local legend, which I always trust, asserts that they mark the graves of certain soldiers in Burgoyne's army, which did indeed retreat over these very hills. It may be, then, that the names of these men were not known; and yet in that case why should there be any stones at all? Because, as I think, it was felt that so much is always due from the living to the dead, even when the dead man is an invading enemy. So the ancient Greeks felt, and so did the farmers of Connecticut a century and a half ago. The names did not matter, but something to stand up and represent the departed, something for them to climb into and inhabit, something for the mysterious gods who inform matter and make it work to hold fast to — this was felt to be indispensable.

There is further evidence, not conclusive but cumulative in effect, of this same feeling about stones to be gathered in almost any New England graveyard where one can read the spiritual record of our last two hundred and fifty years.

The Stones of the Place

Here is a library of stone leaves, unmistakable in meaning when one has learned the easy language, which hardly anyone has yet taken the trouble to decipher. The beauty and power of the better headstones, the theological and cultural history implicit in them, and the unmistakable indications they bear of our steady deterioration are not to my present purpose. What I wish to point out is the fact that, until the French and pagan style of the cinerary urn and weeping cypress came up the rivers about the year 1790, the frequent effort of the men who made this mortuary sculpture was to represent symbolically or — in later examples — with all possible realism the present state of the departed. This effort was often ludicrously crude, but it was also often startling. It ranges from skulls and crossbones and recumbent skeletons to the familiar winged cherubs with two mouths — one that of the risen soul and the other that of the dead body. Not infrequently the coffin itself, with its occupant, is carved on the stone. All this, much too intricate and difficult for a brief statement, I cannot help attributing to a vague sense not unlike that of the ancient Egyptians, that the spirit of the dead somehow entered into the portrait statue placed at the entrance of the tomb. In spite of many difficulties, the New England stones were often appropriate to the deceased. In a tiny graveyard near Stonington, Connecticut, there is a great rough block of granite, eight feet by two by two, that was laid there in the seventeenth century over the body of one of the founders of the town. This is a "wolf stone," and its primary utility was just what the name indicates, but the town kept alive for two hundred years a legend that a giant had been buried there. Not long ago that grave was opened. The coffin was found to be seven feet long.

It may be, then, that this old feeling is not entirely lost. Wordsworth may have felt some thrill of it when he wrote about the huge stone

sometimes seen to lie
Couched on the bad top of an eminence...
So that it seems a thing endued with sense.

The Cabin Down the Glen

Even in Connecticut we show some vestige of it in calling a certain terminal moraine "The Devil's Hopyard" and also in referring to a wild river gorge not far from me as "Satan's Kingdom." These names were given in accordance with our charming Christian custom of attributing to demons all the mighty deeds which the pagan world had thought the work of the gods. In England to this day most prehistoric monuments of stone are ascribed by country folk to Grim, that is, the Devil, and the farmers of Connecticut explain the large numbers of stones in their fields by saying that the Devil threw them over from Long Island.

For my part, I find that the ancient realization of the holiness of stones is slowly coming back to me as I myself grow quieter on the surface and more active within. I shall be fully "in league with the stones of the field" when I can say with Francis Thompson:

> *No hill can idler be than I;*
> *No stone its inter-particled vibration*
> *Investeth with a stiller lie...*
> *From stones and poets you may know*
> *Nothing so active is as that which least seems so.*

And in the meanwhile, I find myself growing every day more paleolithic. Why use wood or other perishable materials, I ask myself, when stone lies so ready at hand? And again, why take the trouble to chip and shape stone — especially as I do not know how, and it would take me years to learn — when a little longer searching always discovers precisely what one wants or, at any rate, something that will do. With patience and skill and an accommodating imagination, almost anything can be found in an old stone wall. There are black and white stones in it, stones gray and rosy, stones green and golden. There are stones of every shape. Does one want a hearthstone, a chimney cap, a stair, a stepping stone, a bench, a table, a doorsill, a hammer, a candlestick, an inkwell, a paperweight, a door guard, a bread tray, a fire-dog, or something to throw

The Stones of the Place

at a bird-hunting cat? It is in the wall. So men thought in the old stone days, and in their way they were wise men.

Some years ago, while wandering among the hills of South Devon, I stumbled upon a deserted village of huts that was built at least forty centuries ago entirely of unshaped stones. This was Grimspound, or the Devil's Enclosure, so-called because the shepherds round about cannot believe that the great long stones composing the walls of the circular huts could have been brought and set up there without supernatural aid. Eight and ten feet tall, they are all standing erect after ages of wind and rain and frost to speak well of the men who mastered them. In nearly every hut there was a firestone still to be seen, and in a few I found marks of the smoke that curled up here before the time of Moses. The roofs of boughs were gone, of course, and so was the mud that once filled the crevices; but the stones had a friendly look, and it was easy to see that men and women and children had lived a recognizably human life among them. And what was most interesting of all to me about Grimspound was that it could not possibly have been defended against human enemies, for it lay on the steep slope of a great hill, and its only water supply was half a mile below. An encircling wall it did have, to be sure, but that was to keep out the wolves and to impound domestic animals. These people of Grimspound, then, had no human enemies. They were men of peace. And they built their household gods into the houses themselves. I think respectfully of these men.

But I think more respectfully still of the men who made the stone walls of New England. I am sure that there were giants in those days. We talk of the Old Stone and the New Stone Ages, as Sir John Lubbock taught us to do, but never of the Stone Wall Age or of the Stone Wall Men. I think I know a way, however, in which they could be brought back into some repute. I should like to take a group of contemporary New Englanders into a typical Connecticut pasture, where there is only just room for the goldenrod between the rocks, and set them to work for one good hour pulling up the smaller and more detachable stones. These I should ask them to carry for a few feet and to pile in

The Cabin Down the Glen

a line, trying to drop as few of the larger ones as possible upon their toes. An hour of this would suffice. Then I should ask them to look at almost any stretch of old wall in the neighborhood, expecting them to see it with enlightened eyes. They would be told that the stones in it weigh from ten to a hundred times as much as those with which they had just struggled, and also that there are many thousands of miles of such old walls as this in Connecticut alone.

They were not made for beauty, nor primarily for enclosures, but chiefly in order to clear the land in fields and pastures where, as it used to be said, the sheep all developed sharp noses by trying to nibble between the stones. Like all honest work done with simple materials, however, the stone walls of New England have a noble beauty which is not to be improved by our meddling. Millionaires and other such human nuisances have taken recently to tearing them apart and putting them together again in neater arrangement with flat faces and a coping of concrete. The only sensible thing is to let them alone, realizing that they were built by men who knew how such things should be done. So treated, they are a characteristic glory of the land, taking the place of Old England's hedges and serving quite well for the plants and animals that can find no other shelter. The hedgehog and woodchuck love them. They are the favorite lodging of the sleek swift chipmunk. Goldenrod and aster and wild grape delight in their hospitable warmth, and the apple tree in flourish is never lovelier than when she is sprinkling silver down upon them. They stitch New England together. Without them I should expect her to fall apart.

EARTH-BORN

No lapidary's heaven, no brazier's hell for me,
For I am made of dust and dew and stream and plant and tree;
I'm close akin to boulders, I am cousin to the mud,
And all the winds of all the skies make music in my blood.

I want a brook and pine trees, I want a storm to blow
Loud-lunged across the looming hills with rain and sleet and snow;
Don't put me off with diadems and thrones of chrysoprase,
I want the winds of northern nights and wild March days.

My blood runs red with sunset, my body is white with rain,
And on my heart auroral skies have set their scarlet stain;
My thoughts are green with springtime; among the meadow rue
I think my very soul is growing green and gold and blue.

What will be left, I wonder, when Death has washed me clean
Of dust and dew and sundown and April's virgin green?
If there's enough to make a ghost, I'll bring it back again
To the little lovely earth that bore me, body, soul, and brain.

HUSH! WE ARE OBSERVED!

While I stood at my cabin door just now, thinking of nothing, looking at nothing in particular, the chipmunk who lives beneath the boulder on which my cabin stands suddenly appeared and stared at me.

He does everything suddenly and by jerks, this amusing sleek brown neighbor, with no more real continuity than that of a movie film. He explodes from his hole when he comes out for an airing, and when he returns he explodes back into it again. Like a telegraphic message, he seems to be composed entirely of dots and dashes. Thus, while he is running along the intricate pathways of an old stone wall, I see him one moment as a wavy leaping line, and in an instant he is attenuated to a mere squeak. Also, there are many long intervals during which he drops, so far as I am concerned, into nonexistence. For days at a time I forget him, wash my mind of him, let him sink below the unicorn, while I go on living as though there were no chipmunks anywhere. How he manages to maintain his being across such times of my forgetfulness is a question that staggers metaphysics, but somehow he does, amazingly. For there comes a time when I am thinking of him least of all and — there he is again! He has darted back out of mere nothing into the here and now, as unicorns so seldom do; his time dimension and mine once more intersect; he stands before me, round eyed and immobile as though carved in stone, indisputably a fact, and one to be accounted for.

My neighbor shows a great earnestness and concentration of purpose in everything he does; but most earnestly of all, he stares. The blank astonishment of his gaze says to me: "What! Are you still there? I thought I had forgotten you, dropped you down forever among the mythological animals. How have

Hush! We are Observed!

you managed to exist day after day while I have been busy with other things?" So then it is my turn to assert my actuality, to stand up courageously against his unbelief, until, just when I am concluding that he intends to stay forever, all at once he is gone, erased, the space he occupied one moment before having been instantaneously emptied of chipmunk.

There is something ludicrous about these jack-in-the-box exits and entrances, but also there is a suggestion of mystery. They startle me and make me laugh; and, besides that, they make me wonder. Time and again, after my neighbor has vanished into thin air, I have walked up and down beside the cabin, swinging my stick abstractedly at daisy heads and thinking about time and life and death, thinking about thought, thinking about this perfectly mysterious moving picture at which we are all now sitting. Perhaps that is what my neighbor does too, during his long disappearances. It may be that he comes forth and stares at me only to renew the evidence of his senses, only to assure himself once more that there really is such a problem. And then he dashes off to tackle it anew. That would be like him.

Well, we stood and eyed each other this morning for a long five minutes, the chipmunk at his doorway and I at mine. In other respects he has admirable manners, but I think he is too much given to staring. It has occurred to me once or twice that he may resent what he takes as an intrusion into this glen, which he and a few other wild creatures had until recently all to themselves and that he hopes to stare me quite out of countenance. If that is so, he may as well understand at once that I have come to stay. And so we had it out, eye to eye, chipmunk versus man. The chipmunk won.

Let me explain. One of the few rules in this childish game of staring-down is that the one who winks first, loses. Toward the end of those five minutes I simply had to wink, but the chipmunk had apparently forgotten how, or else he considered that stone chipmunks do not indulge in winking. Again there is a rule that one loses when one smiles. I confess that I also smiled first, for the whole contest soon came to seem to me ridiculous.

The Cabin Down the Glen

But these things were of slight importance in comparison with the vague discomfort that crept upon me as the minutes dragged along. I began to feel self-conscious. It is a crude and not very accurate way of describing my state of mind to say that I wanted to know what the chipmunk thought of me. He could not or would not tell. Not a sound did he utter, not a gesture did he make, and a face more completely devoid of expression than his I have never seen on even the most expert player of poker. For my part, I was thinking all the while that — barring the slight defect in manners which I was undertaking to correct — he was a charming and wholly desirable neighbor for a lonely man to have. So much I should have been glad to say to him, and indeed he might have deduced it from my benevolent though somewhat stern expression. But what did he think of me? Apparently, nothing whatever. The sudden amazement with which he faced me at first gradually wore away into abstraction and a brown study until I saw that his eye was no longer focused upon me at all. He was looking through me as though I were not there. This was too much, for even the most modest of men feels convinced that he occupies space, however unworthily. When I realized that I was not being granted even so much, I retired from the doorway in a slight confusion.

Of course I had been looked through before. Lions do it, and so do tigers, but their majesty and repose somehow justify their indifference, and we feel that they have a good right to ignore us as much as they can. In leopards and jaguars I can put up with it, but it is one of the things I do not like in the domestic cat. Even while her long perpendicular pupils are still fixed upon mine, there is sure to come over them, after the first few seconds, a distant and dreamy look that ignores my presence as though I were a mere hole in the wall — a look slightly wounding to one's self-respect. We are told that a cat may look at a king, as no doubt she may for a moment if she cares to; but can a king look at a cat? I should advise him not to try.

How different is the gaze of a dog! He looks at you as though there were nothing else in the world worth looking at, and yet he never stares. His glance is like that of a boyish lover, shy and

152

Hush! We are Observed!

vaguely troubled; it shifts for a moment in the dazzle of your gaze, returns, and then slides off again. Does he feel unworthy of our affection, or is it that beauty has become a sorrow to him, as it often does with us, and love almost a pain? There is no answer to these questions, but certainly the sidelong momentary glances of a dog's eyes often show a devotion that may bring tears to our own. I remember meeting a magnificent collie not long ago while I was walking down a country lane, dressed in what he might well have taken as the professional attire of a tramp. He was planted so firmly in the exact middle of the road just outside his house-place that I anticipated, at a distance, some little controversy with him about the right of way. Instead of that, when I came to walk by him he blessed me with his eyes so that I carried with me all the following afternoon a sense of benediction. He seemed to be thanking me in that one look for all the gentleness that my kind has ever shown to his. I wished there had been more of it.

Now and then it is our good fortune to see, in the steady unbaffled gaze of a "lower animal," an indescribable look, fearless without aggression and proud without haughtiness, which rewards us by an offer of equal fellowship for the loss of that assumed pre-eminence from which it draws us down. Such glances remind us of things far back, and also of things deep down, in our human nature. They make us think how recently we too were naked, unarmed, unhoused, at the mercy of summer's heat and winter's cold, when life was one perpetual flight and death came always with sudden violence. They make us feel and know once more that, whatever else we may be, we are close of kin to all Earth's children, born of the same wild mother, fed at her breast like them, and soon to fall asleep as they in her strong arms.

One summer morning, several years ago, while I stood fishing for trout on a flat rock in the middle of a swift mountain river in Montana, I heard a crashing in the bushes and a rattling of the gravel on the bank behind me. Turning swiftly about with my rod in midcast, I saw a black bear sliding down the bank to the water's edge. He saw me at the same moment, but kept

The Cabin Down the Glen

advancing until he reached the stream. There he stood on his haunches and eyed me. The twenty feet of turbulent water between us were enough for him, apparently, and they were just enough for me so that we met on equal terms without anxiety or unbecoming haste. I looked into the bear's eyes and the bear looked into mine — for how long I cannot say, but long enough for the flash of recognition and the assurance of fellowship to pass between us. I can remember thinking: "How much he is like a man!" and perhaps it is reasonable to suppose that he was thinking, on his side, how closely I resembled a bear. After a long pause and scrutiny, during which he probably decided that I was only an inferior and negligible bear after all, he bent over, drank several gallons of river water, and then shoved himself up the bank and into the brush, paying me no further attention. Even as I write these words, I can still see his wild, puzzled, not unfriendly eyes.

The animals standing next to us, our "poor relations," do not seem so friendly. I remember a great baboon in the public park of Milan who stood up and faced me through the bars of his jail with a fierce malevolence which compelled respect, and still more vividly I remember enduring for a full minute the gaze of the orangutan who was then imprisoned — I think he has since died — in the London Zoological Gardens. It was a gaze dulled, but not tamed, by despair, as of a creature suffering hopeless wrong. The gorilla I have never crossed eyes with; and when I think of our cowardly and bestial slaughter of those splendid creatures, still passing as "sport" in some circles and disguised as "science" in some others, I hope I shall never have to.

And then there are the animals that do not look at us at all, but seem to have done so just once, long ago, and to have reached their conclusions. Of course I refer especially to the camel. Whenever one gets to thinking more highly of himself or of the human race than he ought to think, one should seek out the nearest camel and study without prejudice that scornful curl of the lower lip, that high-held nose — who can say how villainously a human being may smell in the nostrils of a camel?

Hush! We are Observed!

— and those half-shut eyes that have seen all they care to see of us and refuse to look again. Very humbling indeed is a camel, thoughtfully considered. Why this should be so we cannot say, but perhaps we had best attribute the fact to the well-known melancholy of the camel's disposition, his natural tendency toward a gloomier view.

It is to be hoped that the giraffe also is mistaken about us and that we have never given him any excuse for that ineffably supercilious expression which he carries about so high in the air. He looks down at us out of his lustrous eyes and through his long curled lashes with a supreme contempt — and if not with reviling, then only because that would take more energy than he thinks we are worth. And yet, of course, it is possible that the giraffe is not thinking about us at all, but about the symmetry of his own shape, the grace of his gait, and the taper of his endless neck. In any case, we ought not to brood over the facial expressions of giraffes.

Elephants know everything which they consider worth knowing, but we cannot be quite sure that they include us in that category. The eye of the elephant has far more speculation in it than that of any other animal. It is an experienced, an erudite, a philosophic eye, an eye with memories and anticipations. Unless I am mistaken, it is also an ironic and a humorous eye, like that of a crusty old man who manages to make all the rest of the world feel uncomfortably immature. Once or twice I have met it squarely, and I have not enjoyed the encounter because it seemed to classify me at once as belonging to such and such a quite undesirable order, genus, species, and variety. While gazing at an elephant and being gazed at by him, one feels at the wrong end of the microscope — on the slide instead of at the eyepiece. One starts out as an observer and suddenly finds that one is being observed. This is unusual and therefore disconcerting. It seems unfair for a beast twenty times one's own weight and size to look at one so appraisingly as the elephant does and with so little indication of being at all impressed. How a whale might look at a man I do not care to imagine.

Neither do I care to know how a snake may look at a bird,

The Cabin Down the Glen

or what may be the secret of that dreadful fascination which draws the fluttering creature slowly down and down along the lines of the serpent's eye beam until it is within reach of the swift and deadly jaws. Even at a distance, this is a painful thing to watch. Only the day before yesterday I heard a growing commotion and excited outcry of many birds just across the glen from my cabin. Instantly realizing what was going on, I leapt for the door. Within fifty feet of me, sprawled at length under a pine tree, there lay a black snake two yards long — moving hardly at all, and yet moving. His crimson tongue flickered in the sunlight like a tiny flame. Above him and about him, darting back and forth and up and down but always nearer and nearer, were at least a score of birds, mostly flycatchers and vireos, all screaming. Two instincts, frenzied fear and compelling fascination, were almost but not quite evenly balanced in those little fluttering forms, and I saw that in a minute or two one of them would be drawn too close by the strange magnetism of abhorrence. After enduring the spectacle as long as I could, I threw a stone, and the snake raced away into the shadows. But what was perhaps most interesting in the whole affair was that the charm he had woven, whatever its nature, was by no means broken after he had gone. For half an hour at least the whole company of birds that he gathered kept fluttering among the lower branches and peering earthward; and even after they had flown away, they returned by twos and threes to look again for the strange monster that had just terrified them almost to death. I suppose that life seemed suddenly dull and prosaic without him, and it may well be that my intrusion on the scene did not make for the greater happiness of the greater number.

W.H. Hudson concluded, after a close and thoughtful study of fascination, that the power of the snake over the bird depends largely upon the bird's mere curiosity. In other words, it is precisely the differences between the two creatures that draw them together, as male to female and iron to magnet. Something of this I feel myself when gazing into the eyes of a wild animal. Vaguely and dimly, I have the same sense of gulf and otherness

Hush! We are Observed!

that the birds in the glen must have felt while gazing down at the black snake; and I feel, too, in a much milder degree than they did, the same conflict of attraction and repulsion. The sensation is not altogether different in kind from that brought on by looking down from a dizzy height. Here is a fellow creature, the subconscious mind reports, in many respects like oneself, having the same elemental needs and satisfactions, breathing the same air, delighting in the warmth of the sun, hating the winter's cold, loving life and shunning death it knows not why. So like it is, and, as compared with a rock or even a tree, so very near; yet, at the same time, so infinitely far away! Decidedly, a strange thing happens when a beast and man meet eye to eye, and I am surprised that so little has been said about it. Mr. Robert Frost has grazed the theme in his poem "Two Look at Two," but elsewhere I find nothing.

Speaking in general, it is uncomfortable to be looked at by the lower animals, and perhaps even more uncomfortable not to be looked at, but we shall have to put up with it as best we can. Although we may never be able to uproot our conviction that this planet, if not the entire solar system and the universe beyond it, was designed entirely for us, still we see that there are other inhabitants and that most of them have eyes — some curious and some disdainful, a few of them affectionate and trusting but far more of them accusatory. This is a part of what we pay for our pre-eminence. Cats stare at us from chairs, horses from stables, cows from the meadow gates, woodchucks from holes in the ground, foxes from their earths, squirrels from trees, hawks from the air, fish from the stream, deer from the glades, and chipmunks from little crevices among the rocks — yes, even from the very rock on which a man has built a woodland house to live alone in. Obviously, in a world so full of eyes there is no such thing as living alone. This one chipmunk, who would scarcely fill my hand, has dragged me back this morning into all the perplexities of social existence. That old cosmogony is forgotten now, which pictured God and his angelic hosts as peering down at us forever through the seven crystal layers of the world-onion, but so long as we have the "lower

The Cabin Down the Glen

animals" about us, we shall never lose the sense that "all the world's a stage, and all the men and women merely players." This was part of the terror that George Meredith found in the Woods of Westermain, wherein, if you "foot at peace with mouse and worm," you may walk happily, but where, at the first sign of quavering, a "thousand eyeballs under hoods have you by the hair."

THE GULF

You at your door this morning
  To bask in the golden shine,
And suddenly, without warning,
  Behold! I stand at mine.

Now eye meets eye unblinking;
  Shyly but close we scan,
And set ourselves to thinking —
  A chipmunk and a man.

With ages to unravel,
  With all their toils and dreams,
Wild speculations travel
  Along our four eye beams.

You took your road, my brother,
  And it has led you here;
I stumbled down another,
  As though on a different sphere,

Until, with thoughts amazing,
  We encounter, eye to eye,
Like twin-born planets gazing
  Across the width of sky.

Why stand we so astonished,
  Bewildered, mazed, distressed,
Both suddenly admonished
  Of worlds we had not guessed?

What holds us thus asunder,
  Small neighbor, you and me
Who dwell together under
  One sheltering maple tree?

But wait! The year grows older,
     The leaves fall one by one,
Light fails, our great blue boulder
     Is crumbling in the sun.

Soon we, that have been single
     So long, shall merge again
Upon the winds that mingle
     Atoms of mice and men.

Ah, soon comes that immortal
     Deep dark of ruin and rout
When we shall have no portal
     To shut each other out.

THE SWAMP ANGEL

Twilight is falling in the glen. Hues of pearl and amethyst are thrown back from every rock and twig and bole. Every leaf reflects a ray from the deepening west. The boughs where the shadows gather, the layered leaves, and all the expectant multitudes of the fern, are very still. Once more the trees sink into meditation, groping down that endless road of thought or dream which claims them every night and all the winter long. So still they are, so breathless, that one might think them carved in jade or painted in a picture. They seem to be holding their breath to listen.

From the gloom of the hemlock grove comes a voice — crystalline, liquidly clear, effortless as lapsing water. First a long low tone, blown purely and serenely as though on a silver flute, spreads through the evening air, and then it suddenly breaks and flashes upward into a fountain of splendid cadenzas, a brilliant spray of bird song. This is the reason why the trees and ferns have fallen still. Silence is being changed into music. The cup of the twilight's beauty is running over.

Again and again the magical strain is uttered, yet never exactly repeated. The singer has found so deep and central a thing to say that he is content to say it over and over, but with no such simple iteration as that of the whitethroat. He has solved the artist's problem: how to be always new and yet always utterly himself. Hear him a mile away across some sheeted lake in Nova Scotia or chanting in the aisles of pine among the Adirondacks: there is never any doubt that he is the hermit thrush — or, as some prefer, the Swamp Angel — yet no one has ever heard him sing precisely the same strain twice. After all his thousands of years, he has not yet discovered the perfect phrase. Evening after evening he strives toward it and

The Cabin Down the Glen

aspires, exploring all the ranges of his gamut; but always, when the full darkness comes, he tucks his wonderful bill under his wing, unsatisfied.

No human artist has ever been more persistent in toil. There are days when he sings almost continuously for sixteen hours, from dawn to dark, and also — a fact not commonly known — he often wakes at night to sing again. More than once I have heard his nocturne ring through the woods on a silvery midnight. Furthermore, he always improves in his singing as the season progresses. And yet we may be wrong in thinking that he toils. Hark, now! Another thrush, much farther away, is answering the bird in the hemlocks. The two are singing alternately in leisured antiphones, each listening to his fellow and then trying to outdo him. But there is no haste, no hint of strife in their singing. Both seem to know that there is room to spare on the heights and that nothing is ever done supremely well except with lordly and magnificent ease.

Each listener to this most perfect song of the American woods may give it what meaning he will — or can. It will be shallow to the shallow, romantic to the fanciful, and profound to the wise. In itself it has no human significance whatever, for we have really no idea why birds sing at all; and yet, as we listen, we can scarcely refrain from loading the song with our hopes and memories. In spite of ourselves, some of us have to ask: What does the wise thrush know? From what wells of confidence and faith does he draw up this peace of heart?

We may be sure, at any rate, that there is no lament in this song, as there is in that of the mourning dove, or such as has been mistakenly attributed to the nightingale. Neither, on the other hand, is there the faintest suggestion of rollicking like that of the bobolink. The hermit thrush is no lighthearted and shallow-brained messenger of good cheer like the wren, blind to all but the sunshine of this checkered world. He sees the shadows, too, and sings them. Placidly contented, blithe, or merely optimistic he certainly is not. He is serene.

At the other end of the glen, much nearer to human habitation, three wood thrushes have just begun to sing, their voices

The Swamp Angel

sounding faintly round the shoulder of the hill. It seems appropriate that they should sing in a company while the hermit thrush sits alone. I hope that I can be fair to them in spite of my own eremitic tendency. During a prolonged saturation in the literature of solitude, I have not found any good reason to believe that poets are improved by lonely living. But how may it be with birds? Listening closely now, while the two songs come from left and right, I cannot deny that the wood thrush has all the splendor of his rival and perhaps even more virtuosity. His tones are perhaps even more pellucid. They are like the lights of dawn on broken water. And yet they have not the poetic depth that I find in the song of the hermit. Although it is not a pleasant thing to say of him, the wood thrush inclines a little toward the superficial brilliance of the mockingbird. He sings concertos. But the hermit thrush improvises for his own ear and perhaps for one other listener — a small brown bird sitting on a nest somewhere near the earth, making no sound.

However it may be with human poets, the beauty of bird song stands in direct relation to the solitude of the singers. The most gregarious birds have no song. English sparrows chirp, gulls scream, rooks gurgle, and crows caw. A flock of starlings produces just the cacophony that one would expect after studying our human arrangements for drowning the individual in the mass — a bristling, hoarse, thoroughly detestable noise, chiefly composed of hissing and beak snapping. That is what comes of trying to say what every one else says. But now, let anyone who has heard them remember the songs of the vesper sparrow, the white-throated sparrow, and the hermit thrush, three lonely birds, and I think he will agree that solitude may sometimes have an ennobling effect. Birds of sea and marsh and river are either voiceless or raucous; those of meadow and field are sometimes fair singers; those of orchard and grove are still better; but the birds of the deep woods sing best of all. In both arrangements the hermit thrush, most sylvan and most solitary, stands at the apex.

It is absurd to call him "the nightingale of America" because he is a far more accomplished musician than the European

The Cabin Down the Glen

bird, as all would now agree if only enough persons capable of judging had heard them both. John Burroughs, who was one of the first to recognize the supremacy of the hermit thrush in America, hardly heard the nightingale so that his testimony goes for little. Keats, on the other hand, never heard the thrush — a fact worth mentioning merely to warm the fancy with thoughts of the poem he might have written if he had accepted his brother's invitation to come to Kentucky. I believe that if the hermit thrush had been celebrated, as the nightingale has been, by the poets of two thousand years, he would now be known as the finest musician among the birds of the world. No better illustration could be found of the fact that the popular recognition of beauty waits upon the discoveries of art. Or perhaps it would be better to say that the nightingale, though a less perfect, is really a more beautiful singer because a thousand poets have made him so. In much the same way, by poets and painters and rhapsodizing lovers, even the beauty of women, by no means intrinsically superior to that of men, has been made.

A strange thing it is, and rather shamefully significant, that the hermit thrush has had no answer in human song. During these three centuries of our struggle in the wilderness, he has been pouring beauty through the American woods, hallowing our toil and adventure, but not one worthy poem has been made for him, to stand beside the score that praise the nightingale. One reason, discreditable in itself, may be that few American poets have ever consciously heard him. Emerson did, I know, and also he found for the bird and song the exact adjective, "spiritual," but he never wrote the poem I should be so glad to have. Lowell, who certainly knew both song and bird, as certainly preferred the more romantic and worldly bobolink. He "would" — and a literary critic could hardly say anything more significant about him in a solid page of writing. Excepting Walt Whitman for the moment, justice has been done to this supreme American voice by only one of our poets, and even he lacked "the accomplishment of verse." Henry Thoreau — accurate in spirit though erring in the letter, as he often did

The Swamp Angel

— said many deep and true things, like one poet speaking of another, about his fellow spirit, calling it always the wood thrush. What of that? The misnomer is of no account in comparison with his unerring truth of the heart. These passages of his are worth volumes of accurate ornithology. They remind me of that old Chinese parable about the connoisseur in horses sent out by an Emperor to find the finest horse in the world. After years of wandering he returned to say that he had succeeded, naming the place where it would be found and averring carelessly that it was a roan mare. Investigation by persons of quite ordinary ability disclosed the negligible errata that the horse in question was, in fact, a black horse, and also that it was a stallion; but in the only matter of importance the connoisseur was right: it was indeed the world's most perfect horse.

There seems to have been some kind of obscure consanguinity between this bird and this man Henry Thoreau. It is as though, at their deepest, they have the same thing to say. Any tone that is struck in one reverberates in the other. They are two strings in one great instrument, answering and echoing. Thoreau himself seems to realize this when he writes: "There is a sweet wild world which lies along the strain of the thrush — the rich intervales which border the stream of its song — more thoroughly genial to my nature than any other." And again, he might almost be speaking of himself and of his own prose where he says of the bird's song: "It is not so much the composition as the strain, the tone — cool bars of melody from the atmosphere of everlasting morning or evening. It is the quality of the song, not the sequence. In the peawai's note there is some sultriness, but in the thrush's, though heard at noon, there is the liquid coolness of things that are just drawn from the bottom of springs. The thrush alone declares the immortal wealth and vigor that is in the forest. Here is a bird in whose strain the story is told, though Nature waited for the science of aesthetics to discover it to man. Whenever a man hears it, he is young, and Nature is in her spring. Wherever he hears it, it is a new world and a free country, and the gates of heaven are not shut against him. Most other birds sing from the level

The Cabin Down the Glen

of my ordinary cheerful hours — a carol; but this bird never fails to speak to me out of an ether purer than I breathe, of immortal beauty and vigor. He deepens the significance of all things seen in the light of his strain."

And Thoreau felt also, with a thrill of patriotic pride, how essentially American this song is. "I doubt," says he, "if they have anything so richly wild in Europe. So long a civilization must have banished it. It will only be heard in America, perchance, while our star is in the ascendant. I should be very much surprised if I were to hear in the strain of the nightingale such unexplored wildness and fertility, reaching to sundown, inciting to emigration. Such a bird must itself have emigrated long ago."

There is a minor declaration of aesthetic independence from which many Americans might gain good sense and courage even today. For we are still colonial in these matters. Certainly one of the most ludicrous examples of our prolonged intellectual nonage is to be seen in the odes to the nightingale written by American poets of the eighteenth century. More than one of these docile young versifiers must have been distracted while he matched his rhymes and ticked off his wooden decasyllables in praise of a foreign songster he had never heard, by the notes of a better singer which he did not even wish to hear. And we have not completely outgrown this ignorance and timidity. We are now reading *Moby Dick*, written by a man whom we allowed to die in utter obscurity, because English critics told us to do so, told us that it is intensely American. We began to read Walt Whitman for the same reason. The reputations of at least two contemporary American poets have been made largely in the same way. I suppose that the best way of getting the song of the hermit thrush rightly valued at home would be to bring over an English ornithologist and to have him tell the truth about it.

But, for my part, I should not contribute toward such a visitor's traveling expenses. And as for the thrush himself, probably he would not care to exchange his lot, if he could, with that of the most famous of all birds. There are huge advantages in

The Swamp Angel

obscurity which he would be unlikely to overlook. Consider, for example, how the Roman epicures made a favorite viand of nightingales' tongues, for no better reason than the supposition that because the bird sang so well, his tongue must be exceptionally sweet. Keats was entirely wrong in one of the most memorable lines of his "Ode to a Nightingale," for the "hungry generations" have most emphatically trodden this bird (or at any rate swallowed him) down. Unless something is done to stop the netting of nightingales in southern Europe — one can still see their pathetic little corpses in the marketplace of Verona, ready plucked and spitted — there will soon be no more music on moony nights in Kent. Such are the penalties of fame, and one could make a telling parable out of nightingales' tongues without much trouble. I rather think it would work out in favor of obscurity and solitude and singing one's songs alone — or to those very few like-minded listeners who may overhear. The music itself may not be sweeter because of the lonely living, but at any rate the tongue of the fameless and solitary singer is not wrenched out forever merely because it sings well — a thing which has happened not to nightingales only.

The best music that has ever come from the nightingale is, of course, that Ode, already mentioned, written with a broken heart and in expectation of an early death by a London apothecary's assistant. I speak of it again because, among its many other wonderful things, it records the real discovery that the bird's song is very old and has been intertwined with human history from the dim beginnings. "The voice I hear this passing night," wrote John Keats under his plum tree, "was heard in ancient days by emperor and clown." He gets that right; and he implies there, without elaboration, one of the most thrilling thoughts about bird song. I do not know that it has ever been amplified, but I remember that as I stood, once, listening to the noonday ecstasy of half a dozen nightingales in the "Vale of Tempe" near Hadrian's Villa at Tivoli, it came over me with the delight of a fresh discovery that the song I heard must be identical with that which the good Emperor himself used to hear when that palace was new. Virgil and Lucretius

167

The Cabin Down the Glen

had heard precisely these voluble tones and rushing cadenzas. So had Sappho and Pindar. So had Homer and Hesiod and whatever poets may have come before them. Our human languages change from age to age, from year to year: we do not now speak the English of Chaucer or of Shakespeare, or even of Wordsworth — but the language of birds does not change, so far as we know or can surmise, by so much as a single inflection in the course of millenniums.

As compared with that of the nightingale, the song of the hermit thrush is likely, I know, to seem recent and lacking in history; but that is because it has no place in literature and also because we cannot make its great age clear to imagination by setting down against it the ordinary yardsticks of time. What the Iroquois, the Mound Builders, or the ancient Aztecs thought of it they have not told us, though I suspect that it would be worth hearing. The result is that it seems to come not out of time at all, but from eternity, and that we may think of it as having always been sung in a vast solitude. For me at least, a good deal of its effect of magic is connected with this thought of its loneliness and separation both in time and space. Pouring up from the glen this evening in the twentieth century, it brings to mind the thought and picture and romance of the old dark never-ending evergreen forest stretching from the coast to the Father of Waters and from the great bay to the Gulf. I see the huge fronds of the fern waving there in the shadows, and the deer, and the red-brown men that wandered under the boughs. Such was the choir, enormous and richly darkened, in which the bird sang for ages before Europe dreamed of America. If I cannot relate him to famous names, I can at any rate place him there. While the first Caesar ruled in Rome, this song was sounding by the Hudson. It rang out across the Mississippi while the Pyramids were building. For thousands of years before the first water pit was dug at Ur of the Chaldees, the hermit thrushes had sung at evening above the very brook now flowing past my door, the very song that I am hearing now.

And after all, though we have not known or acknowledged it, this song has been woven into our history. Taking the place of

The Swamp Angel

the English blackbird and throstle as best he could, the thrush must have made that desperate little band of adventurers at Jamestown a little less "sick for home amid the alien corn." I like to think of how it came to cheer the first settlers at Concord after their terrible winter in the long hill of gravel and of how it sang to Hooker's company on the trail from Cambridge to Connecticut. It may have been the very bird that Mistress Ann Bradstreet heard somewhere in the region of Boston's Beacon Hill and which she called "Philomel" because she could think of no better name. It sang to Audubon and Wilson, to Davy Crockett and Daniel Boone and Johnny Appleseed, to William Byrd in the Great Dismal Swamp, to John Woollman on his lonely journeys through the woods with the Bible in his saddlebags and the presence of God in his heart, to Jonathan Edwards at Wethersfield and at Lennox, to a tall young man from Virginia surveying in the southern mountains, and to a still taller young man mewing his mighty youth in the woods of Kentucky. And then, a little later, this beautiful song that I hear must have come as the last sound in all the world to many a young man dying alone in the fields about Gettysburg and Appomattox. While it rings on, so serenely, so assured, with some great comforting secret in it which I cannot quite make out, I see them there, those dying youths, scattered or in groups, along the fence rails, at the wood's edge, or in the furrows of the corn; and always, all day long and far into the twilight, where there is one lad left alive to hear him,

> In the swamp, in secluded recesses,
> A shy and hidden bird is warbling a song.
>
> Solitary the thrush,
> The hermit withdrawn to himself, avoiding the settlements,
> Sings by himself a song.

We have our American antiquities although we have scarcely begun to realize them, and our birds sing as old a song as any. The song of the hermit thrush is rich with a history

The Cabin Down the Glen

that will never be written or in any way expressed except by what he sings. I cannot at all agree with Walt Whitman that he sings "with bleeding throat" or that his is "a voice of uttermost woe." That is what may be said of the mourning dove. Like the greatest human music, which never really does "yearn like a god in pain," the Swamp Angel seems aware of all we suffer and enjoy, but he has transcended it and risen into serenity. Yet Whitman knew this song thoroughly well, and in his superb chant of the spirit which "tallied the song of the bird," he phrased all that I could possibly say of what the song means to me:

> Come, lovely and soothing death,
> Undulate round the world, serenely arriving, arriving,
> In the day, in the night, to all, to each,
> Sooner or later, delicate death.

> Praised be the fathomless universe
> For life and joy and for objects and knowledge curious,
> And for love, sweet love — but praise! praise! praise!
> For the sure-enwinding arms of cool-enfolding death.

MY NEXT-DOOR NEIGHBORS

Twenty feet from my cabin there stands an infant hemlock some thirty inches tall. In former years, before I fenced the cattle out of these acres, it has been a good deal nibbled by the cows so that its foliage is now uncommonly dense, and it looks at a distance like a small squat cone of dark emerald. Until a month ago I was hardly aware of its existence, for I have too many hundreds of adult and majestic hemlocks about me here to pay much attention to beginners; but henceforth I shall never look at it without respect. Louisiana will hear from this small hemlock, and the twilights of early April will be more magical among the mountains of the Blue Ridge because of its gift. It may grow into a lordly voluminous tree that will dwarf my humble cabin, and my grandchildren may fancy that its huge shadows of afternoon belong to the solid fixity of the planet; yet the crowning feat of its history is already accomplished. Like some precocious genius who produces in childhood a work which he can never equal in later years, from now on its pride must be in backward looking.

My attention was first called to this tree, about five weeks ago, by a small brown bird which I saw coming out of or going into it on several successive evenings just at nightfall, sometimes uttering an anxious housekeeping note with which I was not then familiar. It did not seem likely that she could see me where I sat by my stone table in the deep shadow of a full-grown hemlock, but she was uneasily aware of some human proximity. Concluding at length that she was paying rather more attention to that small tree than it seemed intrinsically to deserve, I made a casual search on the ground under it for a nest — without result. The next morning, however, I saw her fly out, as it seemed, from the very middle of the tree,

The Cabin Down the Glen

and in the same instant I recognized her as a hermit thrush. Parting the pendent twigs and branches, I looked down upon a nest, perfectly hidden, of pine needles and moss and coarse grasses sewn together with thin rootlets. In it were three eggs, pale greenish blue.

Considering that these were the first eggs of the hermit thrush that I had ever seen in the wild and that the bird itself — besides being to my thinking unquestionably the finest singer in all the forests of the world — is to me a symbol of things that go beyond all song, it may be understood that this was for me an "ecstatic moment." I gazed down at those three small capsules of magic with such intensity that I know I shall see them thirty years hence just as I saw them then, pallidly shining in the early sunlight. I shall see them as clearly as Robinson Crusoe saw, to the end of his days, the single imprint of a human foot on a sun-swept strand.

From that moment, I forgot all other trees. Night and morning, at noon and at twilight, my thoughts hovered about that infant hemlock. Whether it rained or blew or shone, I did not ask how I liked the weather but only how the mother thrush would like it. And not content with wondering, I went to see. By easy stages — at distances of ten feet, seven, five, three, and two — I accustomed her to my approach. She always eyed me steadily, with something minutely formidable and ferine in the arch of her beak and the half-inch stretch of her speckled throat over the nest's edge, but only once did she betray the slightest alarm by any motion. That was on an occasion when I went up to her in considerably less raiment than convention dictates, even on bathing beaches. With one shrill cry of dismay, she sprang from the nest and fled. This was of course a mistake on her part, for during all my previous approaches, it had been her role to pretend that she was not really there at all, and now her secret was definitely divulged, as good as published; but I had a shamefaced feeling that the original error had been mine.

If there is anything more touching in all nature than the patience of an incubating wild bird, I do not know about it.

My Next-Door Neighbors

Other birds fly over and flit from bough to bough or sing carefree in the distant wood, butterflies gambol in the sun, the grasses billow down the wind and the shadows of the breeze-swung branches quiver, but she sits still and without a sound, hour after hour, day after day. Her eager instinct to be afloat on the wing is countered by a more powerful instinct to sit immobile. And this is the strangest and most touching phase of the whole matter, from the human viewpoint, that she does not know why she does so. Every stage, indeed, of the maternal process — nestbuilding, incubation, feeding the young, and teaching them to fly — is to her, we must suppose, quite unpurposive, meaningless in the sense that it has no conscious goal or intent.

There were some eighteen days of this patient brooding. It was not absolutely continuous. She was off the nest nearly always when the sun shone upon it, and I must admit that she was away at some other times, late in the evenings, when I personally should not have advised it. Her manner, however, even when she was returning from an excursion on the chill edge of nightfall, was always that of perfect assurance and clear conscience. It was as though she said: "I'm doing this. You wait and see."

And she was right. One warm afternoon just eleven days ago I went to the nest when she was not there and found one of the eggshells broken. From the larger fragment was scrambling a tiny featherless creature which I took, against abundant evidence to the contrary, to be a hermit thrush. It would have been a joy to see that egg first begin to roll and tumble and then to see the beak come crashing through, but at least I am able to report that the first thing a hermit thrush does when he arrives in this world is to unwind his neck — which is about half as long as he is — and to open his mouth so very wide that he seems to be opening most of the way down. I should have liked also to have seen the mother when she first set eyes upon that youngster, for there is such an amazing difference between a smooth grey-blue egg lying quiet in the nest on the one hand and a hermit thrush even ten minutes

The Cabin Down the Glen

old on the other. I do not suppose that I should have discerned any remarkable change in her countenance as she sat on the edge of the nest that evening and examined what the egg had turned into, but surely she must have exclaimed to herself some equivalent of: "Oh! This is something new."

If I do not know what she thought, I am sure what she did almost at once after the astonishing transmogrification of that first egg: She went out into the woods, found there another hermit thrush somewhat larger and more vividly colored than herself — found him sitting pensive and poetic on some shady bough, no doubt, meditating a new cadenza — and said to him, in effect: "Hurry home! You have a wonderful voice, and I have enjoyed it greatly during all these days, but music can wait, and I have something to show you that can't." He hearkened and obeyed. He laid his singing robes aside, as Milton did when his country called. The next morning I found him taking his turn at the nest, foraging for provender and uttering not one tuneful syllable. The forest choir had one perfect voice the less.

One of the shyest of birds, this father thrush was amazed to find himself in such a public place as my cabin clearing. He took far more elaborate precautions in approach and departure than the mother had ever done and often consumed half an hour in sidling from bough to bough and zigzagging along the ground before he could deposit his contribution. I sympathized with him deeply because, in my amateur way, I am something of a hermit too. And yet, after all, I was here first.

When the youngest thrush, some fifteen hours the junior of the eldest, was three days old, I had to leave the cabin for almost a week. Upon my return I found the nest literally bulging with thrush. The singular is justified because, although one counted three beaks and six wild black eyes, the three birds were wedged so closely together that they seemed to coalesce. They had indeed grown mightily in their summer days — and they needed to do so, considering that in less than two months they would have to be on toward the gulf of Mexico, traveling not in bassinets, but on the wing, a mile high, at night, going over country never seen before, without guides, the young birds

My Next-Door Neighbors

of this season flying in separate flocks, separated forever from their parents. Ah, yes; they needed to grow.

It was yesterday that I returned and saw the three fully fledged and almost full-grown birds sitting very still on the nest. They had never taken any exercise. This morning, looking from my cabin window, I saw them fluttering their wings, stretching their necks, shaking themselves as though in glee at the sunshine that streamed in upon them. An hour later there were only two birds there. In half an hour I looked again and there was one. Twenty minutes later the nest was empty. On this ninth of August, then, the little hemlock tree twenty feet from my cabin door finished its task. Three arrows have been drawn from this green quiver. Far and wide in the world may they fly and sing!

RIPENING HOURS

Looking westward from the hill slope in the morning, I can almost see the landscape change before me while I gaze. Certainly it is richer and more various in tone than when I stood here yesterday, and I see that if I am to watch the splendor of the year mount slowly through all its delicate gradations, I must be vigilant from hour to hour. Early summer's monotony of green has given place to the tints of maturity; brown and purple, dim orange and umber are faintly discernible along the lower slopes, and there are rare touches of scarlet from the dogwood and sumac in the thicket. Single trees that I have never distinguished before stand forth now from their backgrounds and claim a separate attention. The cedars far and near begin to glow with their peculiar nameless hue, which is not quite olive as one sees it elsewhere but a sort of olive beatified. Among the solid ranks of the ferns at my feet there is here and there a frond that seems to be made of beaten gold. Slowly, leaf by leaf, yet swiftly too, if the total volume of change is considered, the landscape is turning golden and ruddy, like an apple, beneath these August suns.

Whether the world is more beautiful at this season than it was two months ago would be impossible to say, but undoubtedly we are now better prepared to discern its loveliness. We have grown accustomed to the open air, and for all high beauty custom is a better preparation than surprise. The sky is now our natural ceiling; blown trees and journeying clouds are familiar companions; bees and birds and squirrels are no longer strange to us but neighborly. The open fields, windy hilltops, woodlands, lakes and streams are more homelike now than the rooms we inhabit in winter. We have made ourselves a new home, or returned to an old one, of which the mountains are the walls

Ripening Hours

and dawn and sunset are the windows. At last, then, we are ready to see whatever is shown. These days of later summer may not be better than others, but more than any others they make us feel at home. They warm us to the heart, as they do the apple hanging low above the old stone wall.

Winter in these New England hills is a long stern conflict, spring is a brief ecstasy like first love, and autumn is sheer amazement, but late summer brings us peace. Then it is, if ever, that we pass the bounds of mere admiration for the outer show of sky and field and penetrate to understanding. Then we can almost fancy at times that we see the hills and valleys as the hawk does, while wheeling high in the noon, and the woods as the shy doe sees them with her soft and guileless eyes. Woods and hills and valleys have put off their strangeness and have given us back their fellowship.

Ah, to set out on a walk now, and a long one, through this ripe country of the summer hills; to loiter for three Olympian weeks along lanes grass grown and spotted with shifting shade, where the goldenrod brightens the sunshine and the cardinal flower flows in the cool; to lean for hours over bridges while fancy follows the curl of the waves, and to lean on fence-rails at evening while my thoughts grow still as the corn; to ask my way of no one because one way is as good as another; to drink at the spring and the brook, to eat where the deer browse, to sleep under pines; to be free once more as the tiny glistening ball of thistle-tuft that slowly twirls and drifts and settles high up in the blue of noon; to welcome all weathers because I like them all, and to delight in every landscape because I know that even the fairest must derive its beauty from the beholder, as the farmhouse window shining at sunset draws all its splendor from the sun; to gild all things I see — not the bright and cheerful only, but those that need it more — with a mild radiance shining from within, as though I carried a portable sun in my pocket, or at least a private moon; to find all the things I need and many that I do not deserve because I look for nothing; to own everything I see because I go humbly as one who owns nothing whatever; to study woodchucks and cows a good deal, trying to

The Cabin Down the Glen

emulate those half-wise creatures in so far as they are worthy of imitation — that is, to lose haste and eagerness without losing intensity; to realize that there is time enough for all good things and that nothing of mine can be kept from me; to make my peace once more with the good brown earth from which I came and back to which I go, accepting it utterly and ceasing to wish for any nobler origin or destiny because there is none; sometimes to sing because I am happy, sometimes to talk to myself because no other listener would understand, but most times to be silent because the only things worth saying are so far beyond the reach of words. Ah, to sink down and down into the ancient quiet that broods among the hills, seeking no man's company — and yet, perhaps, to meet my better self someday on a bridge or a brown hilltop or resting beside a brook in the softly breathing woods, and to have some talk with him!

And then to hear the whitethroat whistle once again from some bare upland, though the season is growing late for him; to catch the last cadenza from the hermit thrush on some still evening after rain; to hear the fair-weather call of the crow as he flies high over, roving from wood to wood, making the whole cope of the sky his sounding board; to feel the quiet air of afternoon faintly shaken by the drumming grouse; to be lulled at night by the rhythmic chant of crickets, and all day long to hear in the boughs overhead the drowsily shrill cicada; to sit by rivers and brooks and rivulets and wherever lake water murmurs, listening long and remembering times far back and places faraway; to miss no whisper of the leaves above or of the ferns and grasses at my feet, no note that rises from the myriad shy fifers of swamp and field. And most of all to listen for the solemn music that sounds from the open sky upon those who wait patiently for it in quiet places. Once again, in the stillest night, while the stars are changing their posts of sentry, to hear that far-off splendor of heavenly strings and trumpets that is silence singing!

Now and then, no doubt, one would do some thinking in the course of such a long rambling walk, although one's thoughts would certainly ramble too. For once, then, to think freely — not

Ripening Hours

as the member of any party, organization, institution, religion, caste, class, nation, or club, not as one having a reputation to gain or support, but simply as one man with his center inside himself, answerable to nothing but the truth. Beside some mossy trunk springing from among the asters and goldenrod, to sit for a whole day, if need be, and to settle some one thing with myself, to bandy and toss back and forth some problem hitherto evaded as too difficult or too dangerous, to ask myself the most searching questions and to answer them if I can, to struggle through to an honest conclusion about one of the few permanently important questions of our life. If, indeed, one is to avoid a limp and lazy sinking down into the landscape at this season and is to remain what he should be, *homo additus naturae* [Man/the human being added to nature], it can be done only by such thinking as this, the hardest work and the finest sport in the world.

"Man added to nature" — that is a pregnant phrase of Francis Bacon's and one to which these halcyon days give new meaning. Something there is in a man forever different from stocks and stones. That we know. Yet we know also, and toward the end of the summer we feel with strongest assurance, that the mysterious spirit of man is strongly akin to earth. There comes a day, or a series of days, when every voice of the outer world resounds and reverberates far inward as though through an instrument at last in perfect accord. Earth and man resonate in unison like parallel strings of a lute. As surely as air is good for breathing, this planet is felt to be our home. We are so suffused by the hues of earth and sky that they have come to seem but the many-colored fabric of our own thought. Each new scene we encounter is a familiar place, long forgotten but now recalled, in the deep rich country of the mind.

SKY MUSIC

Whence comes these noble voices that surround
My stillest hours with oceanic tone?
What rapt musicians, ranged about what throne,
Weave wonder out of quiet so profound?
Far-off, beyond the battlements of sound,
Ethereal harps are plucked, blithe horns are blown.
From some high place where Silence dwells alone
Song falls upon me as rain upon the ground.

What grief can be while these vast instruments
Roll volumed thunder on the spirit's shore,
Scattering glory over all its dross?
And what is failure while, beyond the sense,
These multitudinous hallelujahs pour
Eternal triumph on the moment's loss?

NATURE'S SECOND VOLUME

One by one, in the valley below me, the lights are going out in the windows of scattered farmhouses. A lantern gleams and winks a mile away, swinging slightly, as Farmer Taylor returns for the last time from barn to house. Very faintly through the still night air, I can hear the slam of his back door; and soon his windows are dark. As for me, I have no door to close. My lights are growing clearer hour by hour as they climb among the treetops and wheel serenely over. Soon I shall be the only man left awake in all this shadowy countryside to watch with the owl and the whippoorwill. I am going a journey among the stars.

It is ten o'clock, and after, by the planet that has just risen above the tallest pine. Between the glimmering trees to the northwest, some radiance of the day that is gone is lingering yet. How long they last, these pearly twilights of midsummer! Indeed, there is no such thing as utter darkness out-of-doors at any time of year, even under a sky of heavy clouds. Total absence of light is artificial, man-made. In the husbandry of heaven, as in the old times when domestic economy circled round the hearth, always enough kernels of fire are left to enkindle a new day.

Sitting in my camp chair or pacing up and down the forest path under the trees, I become at every moment more alert, more attentive to all that passes without and within. It is as though senses long disused and forgotten were coming into play. Strange odors blow by me like puffs of summer cloud. My feet tread the path which I cannot see, all rugged with roots and crooked as it is, with less stumbling than by day. I hear the little river purling among its mossy stones half a mile off down the hill. Merely by the voices of their leaves and needles,

The Cabin Down the Glen

I distinguish the trees about me. The moving air pours evenly among the boughs of the pine, it rustles in the tall maple overhead, and it sends out a faintly sibilant rattling as it shakes and shivers the leaves of the poplar. Here and there, at long intervals, I hear a crackle of twigs where some small animal, a skunk or hedgehog perhaps, is moving slowly about. Once, and once only, there comes a swift patter and prance of delicate feet among the ferns, going downhill at top speed through the darkness. What was it? A fawn? I shall never know.

A man might travel round the globe without finding the mystery and strangeness that I have all about me here in the woods tonight, within a few hundred feet of my cabin. And moreover, the strangeness of the foreign would not teach him so much or move him so deeply as this discovery of old familiar things in a new aspect. Yet there must be numberless adult persons in the world who have never spent a night under the open sky and to whom a full half of earth's beauty is therefore unknown. Thousands of these same persons, no doubt, regard themselves as lovers and even students of Nature, and to this no objection need be made unless they claim something like full knowledge of the world of the open air; but when they do that, they are like a man asserting that he is thoroughly familiar with a coin of which he has seen only one side. The common feeling that only the vividly lighted day is worth our attention is due to mere ignorance, exactly like that which once allowed us to speak of the "Dark Ages." Night has a suzerainty of her own, an independent domain. There are many flowers, closed to the bee and hummingbird, that send their fragrance abroad only for the moon moth. There are many wild creatures that are blinded by the sun and birds that fly only in darkness. Night is no more a preparation for the day than day is a prelude to the night. We may quite reasonably think of sunset as the early morning of darkness, of midnight as its somber noon, and of dawn as

Nature's Second Volume

its evening. The Book of Nature fills two volumes. There is also the Old Testament, which we have too long ignored.

Those who know only Nature's daytime beauty may know less than half, in fact, of what she has to show and teach. This is not to say that more is actually discernible by night, but rather that there is more to be felt, surmised, and intuitively understood. In daylight the senses are more directly and forcibly addressed so that the mere acquisitive faculty of the mind is likely to take control and we gather chiefly information. Night suggests meanings. Night unto night, as the Psalmist said, "uttereth wisdom." Strutting and puffing about among his little mechanical toys in the daytime, a man may flounder into the conceited notion that he is running things. Alone, at night, under the stars, he may learn better.

Certainly it is possible to walk in the woods and fields for years, even observantly, without gaining the sense of intimacy with them that may come in a single night. To lie under a tree through the time of darkness is one of the surest and simplest ways of making our small planet seem entirely ours. This experience leads one through doubt and back to faith — and surely the only faith worth having is one that has been strengthened and purified in danger and in strife. This is how one finally learns the maternity of earth, if one ever does, and comprehends her vast patience and strength. It makes one become "as a little child." It is like going home.

The recollection returns to me now of a night that I spent years ago under a great oak on Boars Hill, near Oxford. There was nothing to be seen except the dim pattern of leaves against the sky with here and there a faint star, and there was nothing to be heard except the many clocks in the towers of the distant town chiming and striking the hours; but there was much to be felt, and what I chiefly felt was companionship. The firm rough bark of the oak against my shoulder and the touch of a frond of bracken near my hand gave me assurances impossible to express in language. I knew that the three of us — fern and tree and man — were engaged upon one enterprise of which no one of us knew much, that we were of like origin

The Cabin Down the Glen

and destiny, about which we were equally ignorant, and that this destiny was somehow noble, although it would soon sink us all out of sight and remembrance. That night under the oak taught me how good life is on the simplest terms — and, indeed, how it seems to get better and better as it is simplified.

Thomas Hardy, as everyone knows, had a strange power of suggesting the all but complete saturation of the human being by surrounding Nature. In *The Woodlanders*, in *Tess*, in *Far from the Madding Crowd*, and most of all in *The Return of the Native*, there are characters that are like trees walking, boulders that move about, wild heather of the moors that has come down to dwell with man. These people are as earthy as the leprechaun. They are like the progeny of Pyrrha and Deucalion—autochthonous, earth children. And how is this effect made? For one thing we need to remember that it was done by a peasant turned artist, by a man who was born between the heath and the woodland, and then we should observe what delight he takes in showing his people as they move about under the open sky at night. The woods and fields are as familiar to them in the darkness as our chambers are to us. The Reddleman and Farmer Oak and Eustacia Vye are so nocturnal in habit, so at ease with the night, that they seem to belong to the soil like any stump or stone that the earth has thrust forth to watch the journeying stars. And Tolstoy had a guess at this secret too, as we see in the mighty passage of Anna Karenina where Levin is shown passing the night with his peasants in the hay he has helped to mow. The revelation of comradeship with toiling men, and still more with the patient earth, that comes to him in those hours is such as only the night can give.

For the most part people do not know about the night anymore than they do about solitude and silence. They hide themselves away from these things, all three, as though they were dreadful, whereas in fact they are only solemn. Yet a deep acquaintance with solitude and silence and night is all that most people need to cure their petty self-seeking and their strife, for Longfellow was assuredly right when he said

Nature's Second Volume

The fountain of perpetual peace flows there —
From those deep cisterns flows.

How strange it is, and how curious an effect of custom, that even those who care sincerely for the beauty of earth and sky never drink from those cisterns! No sooner are they hidden under roofs and coverlets than a world awakens of which they have hardly guessed, and a pageant begins which is not for their eyes. The very hills of home on which they have gazed a thousand times, so as to learn them by heart, loom strangely against the darkened sky. This is not the same world under another lighting but something different, more withdrawn, more serene, more thoughtful. Rightly considered, night brings no sense of privation but rather one of deepening and ennoblement. The silent looms that weave the world's beauty never linger, never pause. Solemn, indeed, the beauty of the night may be, but it cannot be sad while the breeze is talking among the leaves and the stars go forth on their golden traffickings.

The best nights for sleeping out are those that follow days spent entirely in the open, because when one has been walking or working under the sky for many hours, he is more able to value the accommodations provided beneath a wayfaring tree. Thick foliage above to keep off the dew and the possible rain, a gentle slope to ensure a moderately dry bed, a thick blanket and a knapsack for a pillow — these are the comforts of such nights, and the necessities are considerably simpler. If there be running water within earshot, so much is added for pure luxury. But in fact the whole experience is luxurious. To lie for hour after hour in a worldwide chamber swept by wandering airs, to hear the faint rustlings of earth and the murmur of drowsy leaves, to watch the stars all aswim like so many small silver fish far below in the deep blue sky, floating on deep down there from leaf to leaf and from bough to bough — this is all that any reasonable heart can ask. If one sleeps but little, that is because there are better things to do; and one may remember that an hour of sleep in such a place is worth three under a roof.

The Cabin Down the Glen

Some years ago there was an attempt made in England to enforce an old law, dating from the time of Elizabeth, which forbids sleeping in the open air. A number of gypsies and poor wanderers who had no other place to sleep in were taken up on the strength of this iniquitous law and put forcibly under the roofs of jails. (I did not learn that any wealthy persons who may have been sleeping out as a matter of choice were molested by the police, for of course it is the crime of dire necessity, the misdemeanor of not owning any roof to cover one's head, that the law is meant to punish. Those thirteen companions who walked the roads of Galilee two thousand years ago, sleeping where they could, would scarcely be so foot-free in modern England.)

Of all the intolerable invasions of private right that ever tried to disguise themselves under the name of law, this seems to me the most stupidly bourgeois and Puritanical. To say that a weary and homeless man shall not stretch his length on the earth that bore him and that belongs to us all, under the sky that belongs to no one, and there take his fill of holy sleep is to render the law a hateful thing and to earn hatred for all who make and enforce it. Speaking in general, a foreigner should obey implicitly all the laws of the countries in which he finds himself — although a foreigner who attempts to do this in America will soon go mad — but I am happy to say that I have broken this English law many times, and I hope to do so again. If the propertied classes of America see fit to make a similar enactment, I shall take an equal pleasure in breaking that.

Eleven o'clock has passed, and twelve. It is the full, broad noon of night. The sun is shining upon China now, lighting the paddy fields, gilding the pagodas, and etching the shadows of little flowers upon the stones of the Great Wall. And here comes his sister to light me — an old and haggard moon tottering up among the branches and dropping glimmers and glints of ivory on the forest floor. The woods are transformed

Nature's Second Volume

by her coming into something unreal and theatrical. The trees that were solid blocks of shadow are now filmy, phantasmal, translucent. Caverns and gulfs of darkness are hollowed out. Vistas of gloom are opened, and avenues of mystery. Through the hardwood trees the beams pour down in cascades of luster, but among the conifers there is more resistance. The light falls deeper into the pine than it does into the hemlock, and it is more splintered by the poplar than by the maple and oak. And yet before the moon has climbed a quarter of the sky, the woods seem full of light.

It is one o'clock. The moon has awakened a peewee far off in the shadows, and he utters, only once, that sleepier half of his always sleepy song: "P-e-e-r!" How sweetly it slides down the chromatic scale, like audible moonlight!

Two o'clock passes and three o'clock comes. The constellations climb the pine tree, leap into the gulf of space, and settle slowly westward while I sit here without stirring, or pace up and down, drawing the stillness and the distances into a human thought.

This is a strange experience, waiting and watching while America dips down into the night, as a cartwheel dips into a stream in crossing and scatters the water-drops. Never have I been more aware of the rolling orb, its rotundity and motion. Stars, planets, and constellations moving on from bough to bough give me this awareness as the westing sun has never done. To see the last light fade in the northwest and then, some six hours later, to see it gush up again in the northeast is to make sure that we are indeed going on a vast sidereal journey.

※

One who is spending his first night afield is likely to be surprised by the endless quiet business, the soft bustle and stir, that goes on about him. The dog that bays at the moon a mile away fills the sky with delicate clamor; the hedgehog pushing through the grass near at hand seems to brandish every spear

The Cabin Down the Glen

and plate of his panoply as he rattles by; the breeze loiters from tree to tree with a different word for each; a drowsy bird tells the woods a syllable of his latest dream and then hides his head under his wing to dream again.

And also there is an hour when the creatures and forces of the savage wilderness seem to be crowding back over the territory man has wrested for a time. Sudden cries of birds and beasts one cannot name jar the quiet and shock the heart. Hoot owls circle the dusk with dreadful calls; foxes prowl in the thicket; there comes a swift panic of flight through the fern; step by stealthy step the deer go down to drink.

In that hour a lonely man, though brave enough, may quail, not at any bodily terror but before the doubts that freeze the heart — doubts of earth's friendliness and of her care for our hopes and dreams. It is the superb indifference of the stars, I think, that suggests these questionings. They neglect us, utterly. They need us not at all. We have no part or lot in their majestic scheme. Infinite ages before we were, they began this enormous dance, which will go on for infinite ages after we have disappeared. Thought wanders away into those eons man never knew, when even our homely planet and the half-human fields and woods were roamed by monstrous creatures of incredible scale and claw. This hugely prolific and ever gravid, always careless Mother Earth, continually overlaying and stifling her own young — why should she care more for us, the puniest of her bantlings, than she did for the mighty dinosaur and the saber-toothed tiger? Surely, she does not. Where they have gone we are going; and when we go — ah, this is what tears the heart! — it will not be only our flesh and bone that sink back to the dust but all the treasures of our long toil. The thought of Plato, the music of Bach, the wisdom of Buddha, and the heroism of innumerable hearts will be as though they had never been.

"When I consider the silence of infinite space," says Pascal, "and how mankind is left alone by himself in a tiny corner of the universe, with no light or knowledge, ignorant of how he came and of what will become of him, I am overwhelmed by such

Nature's Second Volume

terror as a man might feel on awaking in some frightful desert island whither he has been carried in his sleep." Yes, there it is — that ultimate and terrible solitude in which the unsupported spirit within us faces the incomprehensible universe without and finds no bridge, no interpreter. "If a man would be alone," as Emerson said, "let him look at the stars." Mind and matter confront each other, nakedly. There is nothing to be done; there is nothing to say; one can only be still, sustaining as best one can the awful pressure of infinite being and the sense of one's nothingness. It is egoism that crumbles first under the strain; or, if that is too strong, then it is likely to be reason that goes. The agony of Pascal before the spectacle of the stars was due to the great strength of his egoism and also of his mind. For most men who really endure this experience, the opposition is resolved, I suppose, either by the mind's surrender, in which it seems to go forth and become as it were "the brain of heaven," or else by drawing the stars down into one's thought and making them wholly "subjective." But these are mere tricks of thinking, devised for escape. Almost invincible is the instinct to find some attitude that will be flattering to the self and will lift it back into its own regard. The baser elements of Occidental religions, as contrasted with those of early India and China, show this unacknowledged but easily discernible purpose, to rehabilitate the pride that has been insulted by the stars. They lose the lesson of humility.

There are two other attitudes, not so much of thought as of feeling, in which we may accept the challenge of indifferent Nature with full foreknowledge that it leads to our defeat. In the one we may remember and say with a deep pride that the human spirit, though everywhere hindered and thwarted, has yet done marvelous things and that nothing, certainly, of all that we know or surmise about the stars or about the answering worlds of the atom surpasses it in beauty or in wonder. And again one may feel that the very frailty and evanescence of our human lives, played out as they are on an infinite stage, to no purpose and with no lasting result, surround all that we do here, and have done and shall do, with the beauty of pathos. If there is always

The Cabin Down the Glen

to be this disproportion between the world and our aspiration, if we are always to be visited by these "thoughts beyond the reaches of our souls," surely there is so much the more nobility in our constant endeavor.

And then there is one more thing that one may do while confronting the stars eye to eye: one may wait for the dawn. Only the eyes that have been washed in darkness can see the dawn's fully glory. Only the hearts that have known how long the night is are made clean for that gradual splendor. To feel the full warmth of its comforting, one must have known the chill of doubt. Rightly to see the sky of morning, one must have lain on the earth. It was to a man who had laid his head "upon the stones of the place" that the vision came of ladders of light going up into heaven with angels ascending and descending upon them — and what was that vision except the ancient and ever-new miracle of dawn?

Four o'clock is approaching. Do I see a pallor different from that of the moon growing now along the eastern sky rim? Are those eastern stars less clear? A change, gradual yet swift, is sweeping through the woods. The moon loosens her hold on the pine. The silver gives way to rose. A whippoorwill, silent since midnight, begins to lash the shadows. He wakens a wood thrush, who proclaims to all the woodland that another dawn has been achieved. Three minutes later the hermit thrushes are in full song; and then comes the rocketing flight song of the ovenbird, going up to make sure that the report is true. When he returns, he tells the song sparrow — and what the song sparrow knows is soon known to all the world.

Dawn, the old and inexhaustible wonder, floods and washes all about me. Watching here on the hillside, I can imagine that this beauty is made for me alone. Who else has seen the first dim pennon of gold in the east or has heard "the earliest pipe of half-awakened birds?" Is it not for me that the distant hills are born again and that the opening day slowly recollects

Nature's Second Volume

the rich wide landscape? The stars struggle and sink in the deepening blue. Cattle rise to their feet and begin to move about in the meadows. The little river that has been to me only a voice becomes a strip of silver. All the familiar world of eye and ear is coming up from the bath of darkness; and it comes ennobled to me, who have shared its deeper mood. There will be left a hue of strangeness upon it, which all the hours of daylight will not wear away, and yet it will be more than ever my home. I have handseled the day, and behold, it is very good! Looking forward into the sunny hours, I say over to myself Job's words of sober rejoicing: "Thou shalt be in league with the stones of the field, and the beasts of the field shall be at peace with thee."

HOUSEMATES

This little flickering planet
    Is such a lonely spark
Among the million mighty fires
    That blaze in the outer dark,

The homeless waste about us
    Leaves such a narrow span
To this dim lodging for a night,
    This bivouac of man,

That all the heavens wonder
    In all their alien stars
To see us wreck our fellowship
    In mad fraternal wars.

FAREWELL

Leave the latch-string in the door,
And the pile of logs to burn;
Others may be here before
I have the leisure to return.

— Bliss Carman

The frost walked last night. From the maple tree that shades my roof, the golden and scarlet leaves are sidling down through the sunny morning air, leaving at every moment a little more blue. No cricket sings. There has been havoc in the multitudes of the fern. Summer is gone, and I must soon be going.

For reasons that elude expression, and yet for very powerful reasons too, we are always reluctant to leave any dwelling in which we have been happy. I feel this reluctance more strongly now, I think, than ever before as I sit for perhaps the last time beside the cabin, with thoughts ranging back over the good months that have been and on into whatever months may come. It is as though I were leaving a part of myself behind, undefended, with the winter coming on, and lonelier by far than the waste where no man has ever been. Will it be here when I return in the springtime? Only a portion of it, for Nature will at once resume her sway. And always there is the question, gnawing at the heart of even the serenest happiness: Shall I ever return? The answer to that question is certain: No, never; at least not as I am now.

My thoughts race forward into the winter and look back. I see a small cabin made of field stone and hemlock slabs, standing alone among boulders on the edge of a New England glen, far from any other habitation. For week after week no footstep sounds on its floor, no hand fumbles at the latch. Snowbirds

The Cabin Down the Glen

rustle among the fallen leaves beside it and jays scream from the ridgepole; rain drenches the shingles, the hoar frost silvers them, or the snow lays upon them its heavy burden. The windows are dark. The hearth is cold. From the bough of a small pine near at hand there hangs a scythe, slowly eaten by rust, and against the trunk leans a rusting axe, once keen and bright with labor. The cabin, the tools, and all the woods about them are sinking back into the old slow rhythms, which human will and ingenuity can accelerate and even seem to control for a time, as we count time, but only for an instant by the clock of the stars.

Now that the human purpose is turning away, Nature proceeds unmolested with her mysterious purposes. She heaves at the foundation stones with the strength of the frost. She pulls at every beam and rafter and sends the field mouse to gnaw at the sills and the fern to push at the floor. For, after all, she is only an "Indian giver." A man may bring together sand and water, stone and wood and iron, calling the result a home, and he may delight his pilgrim heart there with the illusion of permanence, but even while he stamps his foot on the solid fire-stone of his hearth and says, "Here, at least, is one thing that endures," not one atom of his gathering has thrown off its old allegiance. Already the cabin down the glen is slipping back and away from me, and I can easily foresee the time when no keenest scrutiny of the boulder on which it stands will discern that a man once built a home and sat by a fireside there.

For who knows better than I that it is too frail a shell to withstand for very long the weight of the winter snows? In the stormy nights coming on, while the boughs are lashing, how often I shall think of it and wonder how it fares! Built by a wavering and none-too-skillful hand, it is not solidly grounded, like a rich man's house, to endure the attack of centuries. It is only a lodge for quiet thoughts, a shelter of peace, hardly more substantial than the nest that an oriole hangs for one summer from a swinging branch. Oh, be gentle, winds of the winter night!

❧

Farewell

A certain nun who writes to me, now and then, some of the most vivid and thoughtful letters I have ever received, has recently said that time must always be an enigma and often a terror to those who are not "of the faith." No truer words could be put on paper — or any that I less need to hear. I have always acknowledged the truth of St. Augustine's saying that there is no rest for the human spirit except in that greater Spirit, which is its only source and goal; but the mere knowledge of this truth does not bring rest or peace in the storm of time. Ever since I began to think, the passionate realization of evanescence has tormented me, often clouding beauty with sorrow and making love itself sometimes an anguish. In the literature of the world I find no more poignant words than those of Shakespeare's sonnets that cry out against this cruelty —

> *Where, alack,*
> *Shall Time's best jewel from Time's chest lie hid?*
> *Or what strong hand shall hold his swift foot back?*
> *Or who his spoil of beauty can forbid?*

There have been some moments of my life that seemed eternal — moments when I have

> *Felt through all this fleshly dress*
> *Bright shoots of everlastingness —*

but if there are any who can maintain such insight through the days and years, I am not one of them. For daily living the best I can do is to accept the appearance of death and decay as though it were real, to let it sink deep like a sable stain into every thought and mood, so that it invests the world and all its creatures with the tragic nobility of things about to die. And thus, in the thrilling words of Walter de la Mare that come home to me more unerringly than any others in contemporary verse, I

> *Say farewell to all things lovely*
> *Every hour.*

The Cabin Down the Glen

⁊❧

The apparent pausing and deliberation of Nature is of course only apparent. Her processes seem to take the pace of our comprehension, somewhat as the motions of a diver or of a flying bird may be enormously retarded on a movie screen; but we have no reason to suppose that this is their real speed — whatever that phrase may signify. Quite as reasonably, we might imagine the cinematograph of the world moving at a million times its present rate so that the vast deliberate glacier that dug this glen would be seen careering down from the pole at the speed of a midnight express, scattering the hills in its stride and dumping boulders as sand is shot from a laborer's cart. Then the stones of my cabin chimney would be whirled together and pressed and hardened as a loaf of bread is kneaded and baked. Every tree would spring and fall as a fountain that gushes once, and then is gone. The materials of the cabin would be assembled here, and all the work that filled a summer season would be done too quickly to make a clear impression upon the watcher's eye. Moreover, the total future endurance of the cabin itself would flicker by between two heartbeats, and I should see the roof fall in, the rafters crumble, the hearthstone disintegrate, and all that now makes a home flow helplessly down to the mother sea.

"I know what time is," St. Augustine said, "if you do not ask me; but if you ask me, then I do not know." For my part, I suspect that it is a trap of thought from which we may some day escape; but in the meanwhile it is well for us that our sense of time has been adjusted to the days and seasons of our planet and to the span of human life. For thus, although we see and know that Nature takes our treasure from us irresistibly almost as soon as it is given, yet some of us can occasionally ignore that knowledge, as the builders of the Pyramids tried to do, and the men who made Stonehenge. Those were doughty fighters against time. They were losers too, no doubt, but perhaps they never realized their defeat. In ancient Athens, which knew nothing of the past, and in ancient Rome, which could not possibly

Farewell

conceive a future when the Eternal City would not still be ruling the world, the thought of time must have been far less a torture than it is today. The sense of glad release that one has in reading the *Odyssey* is partly due, I think, to the enormous vistas of time through which the hero of the tale moves — he himself never either young or old but always the exact contemporary of all the glory that has been and of that which is coming to be. We have lost that naive feeling of temporal amplitude, and few of us have retained in its place the mediaeval feeling that although human life is pitifully brief, it opens out at once into evermore. We have seen too many Eternal Cities die, and we know too many pantheons of immortal gods that have faded from their thrones. No small part of the burden of modernity is that which is laid upon us by the tyranny of time. It is from this that most of my contemporaries strive to escape by means of speed, in which they dimly feel that they are crushing time and space together; and I too, in my different and older way, have been a fugitive here. I have claimed my right of sanctuary among the old slow rhythms of earth and stars and trees; yet now I see that even in them there is no final rest. The pulse of time beats on as swiftly and the march of the days goes by as inexorably here as in the city streets. Some days ago I found the first fringed gentian of the autumn among the browning grass by the brook. There was all the pathos of time, for me, in that unfathomable blue.

The illusion of permanence is dear to us because our inmost hearts are set, whether we know it or not, upon things really enduring, and for this reason we strive to imagine endurance where it is not to be found. Yet even fancy can outwit time only by fleeing to his brother, space. If I could travel away from earth at the speed of light, carrying a telescope that increased in power with the distance traveled, then I might always see the cabin down the glen precisely as it is at this perfect moment. Not a dapple of sunshine on the boulder would fade or shift from side to side. The chipmunk that is surveying me from a crevice in the old stone wall would never return to his nest. The jay, hammering an acorn into a chink of the chimney, would cling there through the ages, blue against the gray. The maple leaf

The Cabin Down the Glen

twirling down from the rooftree would hang motionless in the air forever, as though painted in a picture.

But today I commit myself once more to the storm of time, not knowing whither it will bear me — except that this dust of mine will not be divided at last from that of the chipmunk and jay and maple leaf, or from the dust of the cabin and of the boulder on which it stands. We are all going on one journey, and in some sense we wish to go.

Farewell to you, then, for a while, you great hemlocks and little birches, you moss-grown boulders and stones of the wall, you ferns and squirrels and many birds. Whether I have been your guest or you have been mine matters little now, for we have been companions at dawn and noon, at sunset and midnight. You have not made me feel an intruder here. You have let me look on, my brothers. You have given me a heartbeat of time in which to guess the secret of your confidence and sober joy. If I should live as long as the oldest tree among you, the faith that I owe to your fellowship would not wear out. Great thanks! Once more, for a moment, I rest this hand that was yesterday only a blowing dust and that will be whirled away on another wind tomorrow, upon the boulder, feeling its deep slow pulse.

And now I must close this door.

AFTERWORD

What of the actual 'cabin down the glen'? Does it still stand?

Shepard's daughter-in-law, Mrs. Marion Shepard could only affirm that the Shepards had owned a cabin somewhere near Barkhamsted, Connecticut during the thirties, prior to her entry into the family. Dr. Jeffrey Kaimowitz of The Watkinson Library in Hartford, Connecticut, where Shepard's papers are kept, suggested that I contact Mrs. Barbara Holden Yeomans of Newport, New Hampshire with this question. She had recently donated to The Watkinson Library the correspondence between Shepard and her father, Leslie Badmington, and had written that "if by chance you know of anyone currently engaged in writing about O.S., I should be glad to hear from him/her, for I knew and loved him too."

When I visited Mrs. Yeomans, she said she had been to the cabin several times, the last and most memorable visit being the occasion of Shepard's fiftieth birthday, July 22, 1934, when, she believed, he was living there alone and doing some serious writing. But she had long forgotten the exact location of the cabin.

She directed me to Mary Wood Lawrence, the wife of the late Williams College professor Nathaniel Lawrence and the daughter of Paul Spencer Wood, long time chair of the English Department at Grinnell College, Shepard's co-editor of English Prose and Poetry, 1680-1800, and his oldest, closest friend. Mrs. Lawrence also had visited Shepard at the cabin and, much later, had occasionally tried to find it when passing through northwestern Connecticut. She could direct me to within a mile of the site of the cabin, and when she started to give somewhat complicated directions, I had a sudden inspiration and asked her to accompany me on the quest. She was delighted at the prospect and the next morning we set out.

Near Riverton, Connecticut, we began asking at farmhouses and were referred to the Renzullo property, on which an old cabin was thought to be standing.

Mrs. Renzullo knew only that there was some kind of structure back in the woods in which her son Mike and his cousin had played when they were younger. Mike, now 17 years old, led us through the Renzullo's very contemporary backyard and into the timeless Connecticut forest. There was a path, but it soon dwindled away, leaving us to thrash through as best we could. I was concerned for the 78-year-old Mrs. Lawrence and tried to break branches that she would have to step over and to give her my arm or hand, but she would have none of it. She said she had hiked in the woods all her life and was leaving in a few days for a backpacking trip in the Sierra Nevadas with her children and grandchildren. After that, I let her follow us as best she could and she did not fall behind.

"There it is," Mike said all of a sudden, pointing to the outline of a roof just visible through the trees. We stumbled on excitedly, down the side of a little ravine and across a brook, and though I had to watch my footing, I kept catching glimpses of a tumble-down little cabin built atop a huge boulder up ahead. I came to a tiny courtyard just in front of the cabin and there, as it had sat for sixty years, was a sizable table made entirely of stone. Though it was covered with a thick layer of pine needles, I knew it was the table Shepard describes as having been lifted into place by five strong men so that he could write essays literally "on stone." When I turned to Mrs. Lawrence for confirmation, she was nodding happily and with tears in her eyes.

The cabin's foundation was made of stones brought up from the brook, and the siding was of vertical hemlock slabs. Inside, the floor and roof were badly rotted, but the great stone fireplace stood as strong as it had on the day it was built. The small windows offered beautiful views of the glen and the brook, which were replete with ferns and hemlocks just as they had

201

been during Shepard's stay. Not far distant was an old stone wall and a tiny spring in an overgrown meadow. We even heard a wood thrush.

I was very eager to see if any of the several species of acorns which Shepard describes having planted on a nearby ridge had sprouted and matured into oak trees; we set out again exploring. Before long we found an oak, about twelve inches in diameter, surely around sixty years old. And fifty feet distant we found another, of a different variety. Shepard had planted his acorns fifty feet apart, and I was satisfied that these were his trees.

Then it seemed that the visit was almost over, and we stood in the cabin's dooryard together for the last time. I had been trying to describe the book to Mike (not an easy matter, as readers will have learned), and now I tried to describe the final chapter, entitled "Farewell."

"He puts his hand on a boulder, surely this one," I said, "and he feels what he calls 'its deep, strong pulse.' He knows that his hand was 'only a blowing dust' yesterday and will be dust whirling away again tomorrow,... he says that he will never come back to the cabin again because when he does come back, if he ever does, he will have changed, he'll be a different person."

A thoughtful silence fell on our little group. "I certainly have changed since I was last here," Mrs. Lawrence said, quietly.

And then we shared a strangely intense moment. Nothing more was said, but I think we each reflected on our respective positions in the arch of life: Mike just starting out at the beginning of his, I at the middle of mine and Mrs. Lawrence drawing near the end of hers. There were tears glistening in Mrs. Lawrence's eyes again and in my own as well. I cannot speak for Mike, but his silence was eloquent.

We stood there for just a bit longer and then, each of us, took up again our separate journeys.

Rick Sowash
Gambier, Ohio
August 9, 1991

Odell Shepard

BIOGRAPHICAL SKETCH

Odell Shepard (1884-1967) was a professor of English literature at Trinity College, a poet, newspaper columnist, pianist and singer, indefatigable walker and trout fisherman, and even, for one term, lieutenant governor of Connecticut. Shepard wrote well on an astonishing variety of topics and in nearly every literary form. His biography of Bronson Alcott won the 1937 Pulitzer Prize. His novels *Jenkins' Ear* and *Holdfast Gaines,* co-authored with his son Willard, were successful Book-of-the-Month Club selections. Books on the the unicorn myth, Connecticut history, Shakespeare, and trout-fishing as well as essays, poems and editions of other writers whose work he admired poured from his pen in the 1920's and '30's. *The Cabin Down the Glen*, written in 1935, is the only major work of Shepard's to have remained unpublished until now.

OTHER WRITINGS
BY ODELL SHEPARD

Odell Shepard wrote well on many topics and in a wide variety of literary genres:

teaching guide: *Shakespeare Questions* (1916)

poetry: *The Lonely Flute* (1917),

criticism: *Bliss Carman: A Study of His Poetry* (1923),

walking: *The Harvest of a Quiet Eye* (1927)

essays: *The Joys of Forgetting* (1928),

mythology: *The Lore of the Unicorn* (1929),

trout fishing: *Thy Rod and Thy Creel* (1930 — long out of print but, happily, reissued in paperback by Nick Lyons Books in 1984),

biography: *Pedlar's Progress: The Life of Bronson Alcott* (winner of the 1937 Pulitzer Prize and Little, Brown & Co.'s centenary prize),

history: *Connecticut, Past and Present* (1939),

historical novels (co-authored with Shepard's son Willard): *Holdfast Gaines* (1946) and *Jenkins' Ear* (1951),

editor: *A Week on the Concord and Merrimack Rivers* and *The Heart of Thoreau's Journals* both by H.D. Thoreau, *The Best Essays of 1925, Essays of Today, 1926-1927* (with Robert Hillyer) and *Prose Masterpieces* (also with Robert Hillyer), *Contemporary Essays, English Prose and Poetry, 1680-1800* (with Paul Spencer Wood), *The Poems of Longfellow, Journals by Amos Bronson Alcott, Irving Babbitt, Man and Teacher* (with Frederick Manchester), *The Best of W. H. Hudson,* and, with others, *The College Survey of English Literature.*

Also available from the Rick Sowash Publishing Company

Books by Rick Sowash:

Ripsnorting Whoppers: A Book of Ohio Tall Tales
Critters, Flitters and Spitters: 24 Amazing Ohio Animal Tales
Heroes of Ohio: 23 True Tales of Courage and Character

CD recordings of music by Rick Sowash:

Music for the Appalachian Trail
Sanctuary at 3am
A Portrait at 50
Eroica
Four Piano Trios
Chamber Music with Clarinet
Enchantement d'avril

For prices and other information, please visit **www.sowash.com**